GLIMPSES OF ANCIENT INDIA

GLIMPSES OF ANCIENT INDIA

BY

RADHA KUMUD MOOKERJI

GYAN

Published by

Gyan Publishing House
5, Ansari Road
Daryaganj, New Delhi-110002
Phone: 011-47034999, 9811692060
E-mail: books@gyanbooks.com
Distribution Network
gyanbooks.com
India, USA, Canada, UK, Australia

ISBN: 978-93-6433-211-8 (PB)
First Published, 1970

2nd Impression 2024

Printed at: Gyan Press, Delhi.

GLIMPSES OF ANCIENT INDIA
Author: RADHA KUMUD MOOKERJI

GLIMPSES OF ANCIENT INDIA

GLIMPSES OF ANCIENT INDIA

By

RADHA KUMUD MOOKERJI

PREFACE

THE aim of this work is to present a broad account of the achievements of India's civilization through the ages in different fields of thought and action. Although the account is planned as a general and popular one for purposes of a wide appeal, it is properly documented so as to conform to the canons of critical scholarship and scientific history. It is, however, to be noted that some of its matter does not readily fit into a chronological framework as a mark of accredited history. This is because of its antiquity precluding from its purview precisely dateable facts and events. Some of the matter, again, concerns larger cultural movements instead of individual incidents of known dates. In such cases, one has to discover and follow the inner chronology of thought, and the evolution of institutions in which it is expressed and embodied. This aspect of the work is treated in several of its chapters. These are concerned more with ideas than with narration of facts and realities. It is to be hoped that the interest of the work will not be lessened in consequence of this lack of chronological setting and the emphasis laid upon the thought that ultimately shapes history itself. The very apposite words of Philosopher Bosanquet may be recalled in this context: "It is easy to exaggerate the value of historical treatment of thought and art. History is a hybrid form of experience incapable of any considerable degree of being or trueness. The doubtful story of successive events cannot amalgamate with the complete interpretation of the social mind, of art, or of religion."

The last chapter is based on an unpublished Note of that distinguished savant, the late Sir Brajendra Nath Seal, and on Sizuki's classical work on Mahayana Buddhism.

February 1961 RADHA KUMUD MOOKERJI

TABLE OF CONTENTS

TABLE OF CONTENTS

CHAPTER I

Vedic Thought

CHAPTER II

Indus Civilization

CHAPTER III

Early Indian Expansion

CHAPTER IV

Foreign Trade

CHAPTER V

Industrial Achievement

CHAPTER VI

Democratic Traditions

CHAPTER VII

Buddhist Councils

CHAPTER VIII

Asoka the Great (c 274-235 B.C.)

CHAPTER IX

Art

CHAPTER X

Coinage

CHAPTER XI

University of Nalanda

CHAPTER XII

Greater India

CHAPTER XIII

Unity

CHAPTER XIV

Linguistic and Literary Legacy

CHAPTER XV

Positivist Thought

CHAPTER XVI

Outline of Indian Thought

CHAPTER I

VEDIC THOUGHT

VEDIC thought is the primary phase of Indian thought and is recorded in the *Veda* comprising the works known as the four Vedic Samhitas or compilations of *Rik*, *Saman*, *Yajuh* and *Atharva*, together with the supplementary and subsidiary works known as the *Brahmanas*, the works of rituals, and the philosophical works known as the *Aranyakas* and *Upanishads*.

The *Rigveda* is the root of the Tree of Knowledge with its many offshoots and branches springing out of it through the ages in different creeds, sects, and schools. It is the earliest book of India and of mankind. As Max Muller says: "There is nothing more ancient than the hymns of the *Rigveda*." But, though ancient, it shows the zenith of wisdom. We see in it both the dawn and meridian of culture, as will appear from an analysis of its thought.

Its first characteristic is that it is dominated by a sense of the Infinite behind the Finite, the One creating Itself into the Many by way, and under an impulse, of self-expression. "He the One wishing to be the Many (*asisha*) inhibited His primary self plunged in meditation (*prathamachchhat*), and evolved into the world of matter and mind, into both of which He entered" (*avaran-pranihridaya-pradesan-avivesa*: RV X, 81, 1). And again: *Sa akamayata bahusyam prajayeya;* "He the One desired that He should create Himself into the Many."

This idea of One God finds expression in many a hymn of the *Rigveda*. One is a prayer straightway addressed to the Deity worshipped in the name of *Paramabrahmajnana* (X 71,

1). There is hardly any religion which conceives of the Divine as Formless Supreme Knowledge and not merely as a concrete Deity with form. In the same strain, another hymn calls the Divine as *Atma anastha* (without form) transforming Itself into Matter (*bhumi*), Life (*asuh=prana*), and Blood (*asrik=sonita*) (I. 46). The one (*Ekam*) is described as *Aja* (birthless) (Ib 6). Another hymn conceives of the *Jivatma* and *Paramatma* (Individual Soul and Oversoul) as "two birds perching on the same branch of a tree (*suparna sayuja sakhaya*), of which one eats its sweet (*svadu*) fruit (of worldly enjoyment or *samsara*), and the other looks on with indifference" (unmoved by *maya*). The *Svetasvatara Upanishad* points to the Supreme Deity of all Deities (*Eko Devah*), immanent in all creatures (*sarvabhuteshu gudhah*), all-pervading (*sarvavyapi*), the Inner Soul of all creatures (*sarva-bhutantaratma*).

Thus the *Rigveda* presents the highest and most abstract conception of Divinity conceivable. Its great Gayatri Mantram (RV. III 62, 10) even defines the Divine as the principle of thinking (*manana*) in the mind of man. Man's duty is to apply this power of thinking, this gift of mind, to the constant contemplation of the Divine (*dhimahi*). Thus there is to be a constant communion (*yoga*) of the individual mind with the Universal Mind which informs it (*prachodayat*) *Rigveda* III, 54, 8 speaks of the Universe as "an integral multiplicity" (*Visvam Ekam*). IV, 40, 5 describes the One as penetrating (*Hamsah* from *hamti=gati*) into the twofold world of Matter (*dravinam*) and Mind [*Nrisat=nrishu chaitanya-rupena sidati iti* (Sayana)] and as *Rita*, Cosmic Law, free and all-pervading (*Satyam avadhyam sarvadhishthanam brahma-tatvam*).

No doubt, the *Rigveda* mentions a multiplicity of Deities that are worshipped, but each such Deity is worshipped in his turn as the Supreme Deity. As Yaska, the great Vedic authority, points out in his *Nirukta* (VII 4), "Owing to Its greatness, the One Soul is described as if It were many,"

Rigveda (I 46) explains that "what is the One Reality (*Ekam Sat*) the Sages call by many names," (*bahudha Vadanti*). Again, "the Sages (*kavayah*) conceive of the One in many ways" (*ekam santam bahudha kalpayanti*).

Another characteristic of Vedic thought is its application to God of abstract names like *Rita* and *Satya*, together with names like *Sunrita* (Bounty), *Sraddha* (Faith) or *Dana* (Charity) (X. 117). This last hymn is the earliest conception of Religion as Positivism or Social Service, enjoining upon man his first duty to feed the hungry as a gift of life itself, for Hunger is a form of death. This idea receives a classical expression in the *Sri-Chandi* of *Markandeya Purana*, offering worship to the Supreme dwelling in all creatures as the elemental principle of a Great Hunger (*Ya Devi sarva-bhuteshu kshudha-rupena samsthita*).

The hymn goes on to state: "The rich man should give unto the needy, considering that riches are like chariot-wheels revolving: now to one man they come, now to another. The foolish man who does not give, has no advantage, as he fosters no friend or companion, and eats alone."

Again, God is described in the *Rigveda* (VIII. 79, 2) as the God of Social Service, "clothing the naked, curing the sick, making the blind see, and the cripple walk about" (*Abhyurnoti yannagnam bhishakti visvam yat aturam premandhah khyannih srono bhut*).

The conception of One God leads to that of the oneness of all life, a most cosmopolitan universal outlook as its natural consequence. For instance, in spite of the conflict between the Aryan and the non-Aryan (*Dasa*) in Vedic politics, Rigvedic thought is liberal enough to affirm that "both Arya and Dasa belong equally to that glorious God (*Arih*) to whom belongs the universe (*Visva*)." (VIII, 51, 9). The *Rigveda* has even a prayer for the forgiveness of sins committed against the foreigner (V. 85, 7). The *Atharva Veda* contains the culminating conception that God is as much of the foreigner (*Videsya*) as of one's own land (*Samdesya*).

(IV, 16, 8). Indeed, democracy was the natural product of Vedic thought, emphasising the unity of all life, the One in the Many.

The *Atharva-Veda* (XII, 1, 1) summarises the essentials of Dharma as consisting of: —

1. *Satyam Brihat*.—*Satya*, Truth, comprehends within itself all religions which admit it as a fundamental obligation. The *Upanishads* state that "the *Atman* is to be attained (*labhya*) only through Truth (*Satyena*)" and, further, that Truth alone triumphs in the end, and not Untruth (*Satyameva jayate nanritam* (Mundaka III, 1, 5-6).

2. *Ritam Ugram*. God is described as the Cosmic Law which governs the Universe and is inexorable (*ugra*). The concept of Rita leads to that of *Karma*, with its inescapable effects.

3. *Diksha* or initiation of the pupil by his Guru in spiritual life. This initiation is the first requisite of religion.

4. *Tapas* or the discipline of *Brahmacharya*, following *Diksha*.

5. *Brahman*, one who is a master of Vedic texts or Mantras essential in the training of the mind.

6. *Yajna* or the ritual of self-sacrifice of various kinds which are well described in the *Bhagavadgita*, such as *Jnana-yajna* or *Tapo-yajna*. The Vedic idea of Religion is that it is revealed by God Himself at creation. Creation originated from the impulse of the One to create Himself into the Many (*Sa akamayata bahusyam prajayeya*), but He had to find out of Himself the material for His projected external creation by offering in a cosmic sacrifice his own *Virat Deha* by self-immolation, and maintaining the creation by breathing life into it. Man is created after God's image and so he must follow his Creator in maintaining his own little system and creation by his self-sacrifice for its good. This self-sacrifice is what is called *yajna* by the *Veda*, and constitutes

the Religion of Man. It is social service to which he dedicates his life. Life is an offering to Duty.

The *Rigveda* is also the root of democràtic thinking. It has made of Democracy a Deity aptly named *Samajnana* or Samjnana, the collective consciousness of the people, the National Mind, to which the individual mind must pay its homage. The *Samjnana* Sukta (RV, X, 191) calls upon the citizens to come together to their Assembly (*Samgachchhaddhvam*) and speak there with one voice (*samvadaddhvam*), cultivating a union of minds (*sammanah*), of hearts (*sahachittam*), of policies (*samanamantrah*), and of hopes and aspirations (*akuti*), and functioning in a common Assembly based on equality as an integral unity and not divided into groups and parties (*samitih samani*). Lastly, there is a call for equal sacrifice in the pursuit of a common national policy (*Samanam mantrah abhimantraye vah samanena vo havisha juhomi*: "I call ye to a common purpose which ye serve with a common sacrifice"). Thus should all live in a happy harmony (*su-sahaasati*).

This earliest conception of democracy was also translated into reality. The *Rigveda* mentions the institutions in which the democratic ideal was first expressed and embodied, institutions which it aptly calls *Sabha* and *Samiti*, which are the keywords of Indian politics.

The *Atharva-Veda* (VII, 12, 1-2) calls the *Sabha* and *Samiti* as 'the twin daughters of Prajapati,' with the implication that the work of creation was to be completed by the democratic process. These two were like the first aids to civilization in which the creation of the material world was to culminate. As the two Chambers of Legislature, they are mentioned as working in unison (*Samvidane*). The *Atharva-Veda* also applies to *Sabha* the significant epithet of *Narishta* which Sayana interprets as 'inviolable, not to be overridden' (*ahimsita parair anabhibhavya*), because where the many meet in an assembly and speak there with one voice, that voice or Vote of the Majority is not to be violated by others (*Bahavah sambhuya yadi ekam vakyam vadeyuh tat hi na parair atilanghyam*). This means that Vedic democracy was governed by the Vote of the Majority. A member of the *Sabha* prays that he may speak agreeably at its meeting (*samgateshu*) and that other members speak with the same voice (*ye ke cha sabhasadah te me santu sasvachasah*). He also prays that he may acquire, (*adade*) the collective strength (*varcha*) and knowledge (*vijnana*) of the Assembly as a full partner of the *Samsat*.

The Vedic political theory was that Law or Dharma was the true sovereign, while the King or the Chief Executive was the *Danda* to uphold and enforce Dharma. Thus kingship was constitutional and limited by democratic checks such as the election, and expulsion of kings and their reinstatement on the basis of their loyalty to the Constitution (Dharma). The King had also to seek the advice of his Ministers aptly called *Rajakrits* or King-makers' by the *Atharva-Veda*. The *Aitareya Brahmana* (I. 40) frankly traces national insecurity to want of a leader or King (*arajataya*) and makes him elective (*rajanam karavamaha iti tatheti*).

It is to be noted that the democratic principle was at work in all spheres of public life, political, social and cultural. Social life was organised in a hierarchy of institutions named (1) *Griha* or *Kula* (Family), (2) *Grama*, a union of families; (3) *Vis*, the canton or clan, a union of villages, (4) *Jana* or the people organised into (5) the *Rashtra* or the State. These institutions trained the people in citizenship in different stages.

Indeed, the *Atharva-Veda* gives fuller expression to the ideals of democracy. It fosters the sense of democracy by means of special prayers addressed to appropriate Deities, so that the people may approach and practise it in a religious spirit.' The root of success in the working of democracy is traced to the moral fitness of the citizens concerned in their habits of unity among themselves in the different spheres of private and public life.

Its foundation lay in the domestic life and family where the parties and partners concerned must cultivate constant concord among themselves by way of an emotional integration. The *Atharva-Veda* enjoins the following prayer for this purpose to the Deity appropriately designated as *Sammanasyam*, the Universal Mind pervading, unifying, and integrating individual minds (AV. VI. 60).

"Let us all have a union of hearts (*sahridaya*), of minds (*sammanasya*), without any ill-will (*avidvesha*), with each loving the other as warmly as the cow its new-born calf (*anyah anyam abhiharshata aghnya jatam vatsamiva*).

"Let the son follow the ways of his father (*anuvrata*), and be of one mind (*sammanah*) with his mother with whom he must not disagree. Let the wife speak to her husband honeyed words of sweetness (*madhumati*) and peace (*santivan vacham*)!

"Let not brother and sister bear ill-will towards each other (*dvikshat*)! Let all speak words of gentleness (*bhadraya vacham vadata*), united in ideals and ways of life (*samyancha savrata*).

"Let the spread of *Brahma-Samjnana*, the knowledge of oneness of life, in every household (*grihe purushevyah*), dispel discord and ill-will in every sphere, society, country and the whole world! (*na viyanti na vidvishate*). Men's minds must thus be prepared for universal peace and brotherhood, for 'War begins in the minds of men.'

"Let the people be not divided (*ma viyaushta*) but with pure heart (*chittinah*) work together (*samradhayantah*) in teams of cooperative effort (*sadhurah charantah*), speaking with one another in agreeable words (*valgu vadantah*), with a common purpose and mind (*sadhrichinan wah sammanasah*).

"Let all be of one purpose (*sadhrichinan*) and mind (*sammanah*) under a common leadership (*ekasnushtin*) in a spirit of fellowship (*samvananam*)!

"Let all have an equal share (*samani*) of water (*prapa*) and food (*annabhaga*) !

"Let all be yoked together (*yunajini*) in same harness (*samane yoktre saha*) for common work and worship (*saparyata*), like spokes revolving round the nave (*arah navimiva abhitah*)."

It will thus appear from the above Vedic Texts that a good deal of Socialism and Communism was held in solution and anticipated in ancient Indian society which stood for the ideal of a Welfare State, and the equal rights of its citizens to the primary necessaries of life like food and drink and to work and employment in co-operative enterprise.

As regards the working of the democratic principle in the cultural sphere, it showed itself in institutions known as *Samghas* or Academies of learned men (*dhirah*) whose discussions helped to evolve the refined (*samskrita*) language of the *Veda* out of the popular speech of the day (*Vacham laukikim*), "like groats through a sieve." They are aptly called comrades (*sakha*) in culture 'who come together (*samyajante*) for developing the truths they had realised in their hearts (*krida tashteshu*) or reached by their minds (*manasho jabeshu*)' (RV. X, 71, 8). Their learned discussions hammered into shape both Vedic thought and Language. Besides the *Samgha*, there was also the *Parishat* at which kings joined with cultured commoners in fellowship in learning. The *Upanishads* mention the Panchala *Parishat* whose meetings were regularly attended by King Pravahana.

Again, we read of learned men gathering at the courts of kings in Conferences conducted in the true democratic manner and method. The best example of such a learned Conference was that convened by King Janaka of Videha. Its procedure was very fruitful. It helped to codify the multifarious doctrines and schools of philosophy into a system through discussions by their exponents, of whom the most conspicuous was Yajnavalkya, while there was also among them a lady philosopher named Gargi who held her own against the men philosophers in open debate. The Conference ended with the award of the royal prize (like the Nobel Prize) to Yajnavalkya for his admitted superiority in learning. The prize was 1,000 cows, each of whose horns was adorned with a string of five gold coins called Padas, so that the total gift of gold amounted to 10,000 gold pieces.

It is to be noted that women had equal access to the highest knowledge with men. Enriched by the royal prize Yajnavalkya returned from the court of Janaka to his hermitage only to feel that he should now devote himself to the pursuit of knowledge by renouncing the World in a total spirit of *Vairagya*. Before wandering from home into homelessness (*anagarika*), he called his wife Maitreyi to make provision for her. Maitreyi first put to her husband the following significant question: "My Lord, if this whole earth filled with wealth (*sarva prithivi vittena purna*) belongs to me, tell me, should I be immortal with it, or no?" "No", replied Yajnavalkya, "like the wife of a rich man will be thy life, but there is no hope (*asa*) of immortality (*amritatva*) by wealth." Wealth is only "possession of means of happiness and enjoyment" (*sukhopaya-bhoga-sampannam*) and of performing expensive ceremonies like *Agnihotra*, which cannot lead to Immortality (*Tena prithivi-purnavittasadhyena karmana Agnihotradina amrita kim syat*). This answer at once decided the mind of Maitreyi who thought: "What should I do with that by which I cannot win immortality?"

Vedic society was broadly based upon a four-fold division of labour among the different interests of national life: its learning and culture; its government, security and defence; its economic life centering round agriculture and dairying; and its handicrafts. These four classes of people are described in the famous *Purusha-Sukta* of the *Rigveda* as the four limbs of the body-politic, as integral parts of society as an organic whole. They are named Brahmanas, Kshatriyas, Vaisyas and Sudras, representing respectively the mouth, arms, thighs and feet of the Creator or *Virat Purusha*. These classes later hardened into castes under the influence of heredity.

The *Upanishads*, however, know of both Brahmanas and Kshatriyas as Rishis and teachers, though normally the Brahmanas were the custodians of learning as teachers. Among the learned Kshatriyas or Rajarshis, the *Upanishads* mention King Janaka of Videha, who figures both as teacher of a learned Brahmana scholar like Yajnavalkya, and also, later, as his pupil. As pupil, Janaka offered to his teacher, Yajnavalkya, his whole kingdom as *guru-dakshina* in the following words: "*So 'ham Bhagavate Videhan dadami mamchapi saha dasyayeti* : Sir, I give you the Videhas, and also myself, to be together your slaves!" [*Videhan*= *Videhan desan mama rajyam samastam dadami* (Sankara)].

Besides Janaka, the *Upanishads* mention the following Rajarshis, viz., Pravahana, Asvapati, Sanatkumara and Ajatasatru. Satyakama of unknown parentage was considered fit for his pupilage by Rishi Gautama. The *Rigveda* tells of a family with father as a physician (*bheshaja*), son as a Rishi, and the mother a dutiful housewife grinding corn (*upala-prakshini*), and contemplates different aptitudes creating different occupations not confined to particular classes (Yaska's *Nirukta*, I. 9). The *Yajurveda* (XXV. 2) is catholic enough to state that "the Veda with its words of supreme good (*vacham kalyanim*) must be taught to the people at large (*janebhyah*), to Brahmana and Kshatriya, to Sudra and Vaisya, to one's own people (*svaya*) and even to foreigners (*charanayacha*)".

Vedic thought reaches its characteristic culmination in one of the minor *Upanishads* associated with the *Mundaka*. It is called *Nirvana-Upanishad*, containing a prayer addressed by a Rishi aptly named *Nihsamsaya* (the man of faith) to his Deity to whom is applied the singular and significant abstract name of *Nirvana*. The worshipper of this Divinity has his appropriate disciplines and accomplishments. He must live on alms (*bhikshasi*) obtained without any plan (*akalpita*). He is to wear the bark of trees, deer-skin, and loin-cloth as an *Udasin* (devoid of worldliness). This austerity produces in him certain inner developments. He becomes a *Hamsachara*, one who penetrates into the minds of all (*sarvabhutantaravarti*) and has an insight into their thoughts and words (*mano-vag-gocharah*). He lives in a state of Bliss (*Ananda-matham*). His Deity is also worshipped as *Advaita-Sadananda*, the One Supreme God of Bliss Who is self-shining (*Svaprakasa*). He uproots the objective in him, and burns up his desires, and sense of ego (*prapancha-chhedanam maya-mamata-ahamkara-dahanam*). He is to study (*adhita*) religious texts in the two *asramas* of *Brahmacharya* and *Vanaprastha* as steps towards *Sannyasa* by complete renunciation (*sarva-vinyasa*). The *Sannyasi* must be learned in the *Sruti* and not illiterate. The supreme fruit of this austere *sadhana* of *Nirvana-upasana* is not the anti-social aloofness of a towering eminence from suffering humanity but the overwhelming romance of a universal compassion in which the devotee revels as in his element (*karuna-kelih*). He finds his highest happiness in helping others to whom he feels bound in ties of love!

It may be noted that the three key-words of Buddhism are all derived from the *Veda*: (1) *Samgha* (2) *Nirvana* and (3) *Karuna*, attributed to the Bodhi-sattva in *Mahayana* Buddhism. Buddhism also owes to the Vedic work *Satapatha Brahmana* the terms *Arhat* and *Sramana*.

CHAPTER II

INDUS CIVILIZATION

VEDIC civilization believed more in monuments of thought than in material monuments for which ancient Egypt was famous. But, lately, archaeological excavations have brought to light the material remains of an early phase of Indian civilization in the Indus Valley and some places to its west and east. Its sites number more than eighty.* Its western limit was the port town of Suktagen-dor about 300 miles from Karachi, and eastern, Rupar on Upper Sutlej. Within this area there are found remnants of small village settlements and their cultures, at places like Quetta, Amri, Zhob, Kulli and so forth and their culmination at three centres known as Chanhu-daro and Mohenjo-daro on the Indus, and Harappa on the Ravi. Mohenjo-daro and Harappa are like the twin capitals of an organized civilization, although they are about 400 miles apart. Seven successive strata of antiquities have been unearthed at Mohenjo-daro and six at Harappa. They record remarkable progress in civilization for that early age.

---

* Its beginnings were discovered by an archaeological expedition from New York at sites like Kili Gul Mohammed in Baluchistan dated to about 3550 B.C. showing bones of humped bull and horse but no pottery. The next later sites are Rana Ghundai I, II and III showing pottery, hand-made and wheel-made, and also *painted*, black on red, figuring horned bull, and showing bones of humped bull, followed by buff and red-coloured pottery continued at later sites like Amri, Nal, and Zhob.

This culture extended over a wide area up to Rupar in the east on the Sutlej; to Lothal on the western coast in Saurashtra and to Broach and Surat in the south. Of these, *Lothal* is rich in old remains revealing underground drainage system with its man-holes,

There is a view advanced by plant geneticists that the Indus Civilization was the earliest in the World. The origin of civilization is traced to the origin of food, which sustains it. Wheat is such food, especially its variety which contains 43 pairs of chromosomes in its nucleus, and has the highest food value. This variety originated "in the fold between the Hindukush and Himalaya" and in the uplands of the Punjab, whence it spread to the west and built up its civilization. Indeed, civilization began where cereals and cattle were first domesticated. The wheat which was used at Mohenjo-daro is the ancestor of the modern wheat used in the Punjab. Like wheat, India also first produced cotton as the best material for human clothing.

The Indus civilization presents marks of notable progress. Its two cities were constructed like forts on a *citadel* protected by a massive inner rampart of brick. It measured 460 yards × 215 yards at Harappa. Both cities had big granaries. The one at Harappa measured 168 feet × 135 feet × 23 feet. The *granary* was needed to store up grain, as taxes were paid in kind. Economic Life was advanced

---

soakage jars, cess-pools at regular intervals, and sluice-gates at the end of long drains. The drains were cleared by the municipal body as its duty. There have been also found *Seals* with figures of Indus script and animals, of a dancing female in copper, a dog, a guerilla, a man with a square-cut Assyrian beard, and the figure of an Egyptian mummy pointing to the foreign contacts of the port. There are also found kiln-burnt bricks for building dockyards for purposes of sea-borne trade with countries like Egypt and Mesopotamia. The dockyard was equipped with a spill-channel, water-locking arrangement, and an entrance for ships. A short wall was built for retaining water within the dockyard so that ships could escape from the high tides for loading and unloading. The required water-level was maintained by wooden logs and doors. There are also found clay models of country craft without rails, a ship with sail for foreign trade and of bullock cart. Seals were of copper, bronze and terracotta and showed figures of elephants, bull, unicorn, ram, rhino, dog, stag, antelope, snake, and birds like swan, crane and peacock.

It may also be noted that sites like Hastinapura and Kosambi show continuity of Harappan culture, while Nagarjunikonda in the south has brought to light remains of early ages, Neolithic, Palaeolithic and Chalcolithic.

by means of *transport*, wheeled carts and boats. Chanhudaro even used a four-wheeled wagon.

Pottery was a marked feature of this civilization. "The black-on-red painted decoration illustrates best the unity, originality, and antiquity of the Indian Civilization and is found with complete uniformity from Amri to Harappa" (Gordon Childe, *New Light on the Most Ancient East*, p. 181).

But a very singular characteristic of this civilization was its *Seals* of which more than 2000 have been found so far. They bear inscriptions not yet deciphered. Their script is supposed by Langdon to be the source of Brahmi script. The seals also bear life-like figures of the animals then known. These are Lion and Tiger, Rhino and Bear, Jackal and Wolf, Deer and Barasinha, Sambhur, Elephant, and Bison, Humped Bull and Buffalo, Sheep and Ram, and Fowl. Skeletal remains are found of Camel, Sheep, and *Horse*, Dog, Monkey, and Hare, Goat and Pig. At Rana Ghundai have been found teeth of Horse in its lowest or earliest stratum. Most of these wild animals were the denizens of forests which grew in a region that was well-watered. The same climatic fact is proved by aquatic life represented by crocodile, tortoise, fish and water-buffalo on the seals. The forests also supplied the timber for the kilns in which the bricks for building were fired.

A unique feature of the civilization was its *town planning* and underground *drainage*. Roads were wide enough for vehicular traffic. Their width ranged between 14 and 33 feet. House-drains emptied themselves into street drains by earthenware pipes. They were cleaned through man-holes with covers made of lime-stone of Sukkur. The city's sewage finally found its way into soak-pits, and ultimately into the river. This *town-planning* was thus inspired by a regard for sanitation and public health, as contrasted with the aristocratic architecture which made so much of the temples, tombs, and palaces of kings in Mesopotamia and Egypt.

This civilization was also up to constructing (1) a college building measuring 230 feet × 78 feet, (2) a pillared hall 90 feet × 90 feet to serve the municipality (3) a public bath-house 108 feet × 108 feet with a swimming bath 40 feet × 24 feet × 8 feet, with provision for its filling and draining and (4) the big state granary aforesaid.

This civilization was mainly built up on the basis of trade by which it obtained its materials from places far and near. There were ornaments of gold which came from the Kolar Gold Fields of Mysore as its only source from the fact that it showed the same composition in containing 11% silver alloy (electron). Similarly, green stone was derived from Doddabetta of the Nilgiris and found its way as far as Ur in Mesopotamia. The yellow stone came from Jaisalmir, and tin from Hazaribagh mines. Materials were also obtained by trade from foreign countries: e.g., Lapis Lazuli from Badakshan, Turquoise from Khorasan and Jadeite from the Pamirs and Tibet.

It will thus appear that the commerce in those ancient days covered a wide field. Caravans were proceeding all the way from Mesopotamia, across many a mountain and desert, into the interior of India for its products, while, internally, the North and South in India were bound by ties of brisk commercial and cultural intercourse, overcoming the barriers of the Vindhyas and Dandakaranya.

Scholars are agreed that this early Indian civilization of the Indus, like the early civilizations of the Nile, Euphrates, and Tigris, was an indigenous, individual, and independent growth in many ways, as specially proved by its religious symbols. Some of the seals, for instance, bear figures of Hindu deities such as (1) four-armed Brahma or Vishnu, (2) standing *Yogis* and (3) Siva Pasupati figured as a three-faced seated Yogi surrounded by animals. There is also found an image in stone of a *Yogi* with his eyes fixed on the tip of the nose as an aid to concentration as prescribed by the Hindu *Yoga* system. The Hindu cult is also illustrated in the figures on the seals of the primeval Mother Goddess, bulls, phalli and rings. The importance attached to bath suggests the Hindu religious practice of purificatory bath before worship.

The makers of this early civilization are supposed to be Dravidians described in the *Rigveda* as *Anaryas* or *Dasas*, snubnosed (*anasa*), dark-skinned (*krishna-tvak*) and of dusky brood (*krishna-garbhah*). The *Rig-Veda* condemns them as phallus-worshippers (*sisna-devah*). But it credits them with urban culture centred in its cities of stone (*asmamayi*) and metal (*ayasi*) which had to be stormed by the Aryan God Indra as *Purandara*.

The age of this civilization is inferred from some foreign evidence. Five Indian seals bearing the Indus script and the Indian humped bull are found at certain early sites in Elam and Mesopotamia in strata connected with the pre-Sargonid era, i.e., before 2700 (or 2400) B.C. These seals belong to the later layers of Mohenjo-daro, of which the beginnings should be dated to about 3500 B.C. as opined by Sir John Marshall. Another Indian seal bearing the figures of Indian animals, elephant and rhino, is found along with a Babylonian seal at Eshnunna near Baghdad, which names the Akkad king Shur-dur-ul who lived about 2500 B.C. Thus the Indian seal should have reached Eshnunna before 2500 B.C.

On the basis of a comparative study of the Indus Civilization along with other allied early civilizations like Sumer and Elam, it appears that these civilizations are linked together by a common element. It is their painted pottery marked by the same features, such as the sun-symbol or river-patterns. But the Indus Civilization later achieved far greater advance than Sumer and Elam by its town-planning, metal-working, and sculpture. Harappa also had its plant-designs on its pottery, which were indigenous. Most Harappan objects are unmixed local products. The individuality of Harappan culture is also expressed in its *seals* which show figures of animals not seen on its pottery, animals like rhino, tiger, water-buffalo, crocodile, and elephant, except only one humped ox also appearing on pottery. Humans with upraised hands are seen on seals, while these are also seen on western pottery. But Indian contact with Sumer did not bring to India its cylindrical seals. Harappans were unreceptive to foreign innovations in their many arts and crafts, although the Indus Valley acted as the host to immigrants or invaders from the increasingly desiccated lands of Iran and Mesopotamia, and was thus exposed to foreign influence.

It is, however, to be noted that while the main developments of Harappan culture were independent, indigenous and urban, its origin was due to foreign factors and influence. It was due to the immigration of peasant-farmers from the West who first founded agricultural settlements in Sind, carrying with them the potter's wheel, and found Indians in the mesolithic stage, hunting, food-gathering, with the men herding goats and cows, and women engaged in digging-stick cultivation of small plots. It seems that mesoliths continued in use in India long after the introduction of pottery.

Thus the cultural progress of man in India was stimulated by these immigrants and invaders from the West, from countries like Akkad, Elam, Sumer, and Iran. The Indian aboriginals still survive as speakers of Munda or Kol and are now known as Hos, Santals, Sabaras, Bhuiyas, Bhils, Korkus etc. who form the basic pre-Aryan and pre-Dravidian population of India.

The economic revolution from food-gathering to peasant-farming coupled with the use of pottery is the product of this western invasion. The chronology of pottery shows that its earliest specimen was a red ware decorated in black with designs of animals, humans, and ibex-hunters. The arrival of these peasant-potters from Iran was followed by individual pottery industries at certain sites like Nundara and Amri in India, from which they spread. The bulls of the Kuli culture pottery and on some Harappan wares indicate foreign contacts from 2500 B.C. These foreign early communities were ibex-hunters who spread themselves from central Iran to Sind and formed an important link between the west and east.

In India, they confronted the urban civilization of the Indus Valley as centred at Mohenjo-daro and Harappa, and spread over a vast area from Gujarat to Rupar on the Sutlej, as already stated.

We may now reiterate the main elements of this Indus Civilization which was far in advance of the original peasant-farming communities who helped in India's economic advance in the beginning and in the earliest stage. We have already seen that its main features were town-planning and building in burnt bricks in well-planned blocks on straight main street. There was also "an elaborate drainage system far in advance of anything to be found in the east at that time or even at the present day in all but the largest most progressive cities". (Gordon: *the Prehistoric Background of Indian Culture*). There were also other elements of culture, a Script, a system of Weights and Measures, and a standard of Metallurgy. Axes of copper and bronze were used for felling and splitting the timber that was used for fixing the bricks and roofing the houses.

It has also been assumed that considering the speed of growth of the Indus Civilization it was due to the impetus imparted to it by other foreign immigrants who came by way of the sea. But that does not mean that, in view of its achievements, it could have arrived from some region outside India. It was primarily built up with the surplus of agriculture of which the progress is seen in its remarkable capacious *granaries* equipped with ventilation to keep the grain in good condition. Harappa places the coolie lines close to the granaries for facility for pounding the grain into flour.

These early people's knowledge of metallurgy is shown by the use of bitumen as a water-resisting substance. It was a rock asphalt which had to be refined by the use of wood-fuel in plenty, and was also used in Sargonid Mesopotamia. In the same Sargonid period of Akkad from 2500 B.C. there has been found at Mesopotamian sites plenty of seals of Indus type.

CHAPTER III

EARLY INDIAN EXPANSION

INDIAN civilization was not always contained within its natural, geographical limits. It tended to spread and extend beyond them. An early example of this extension has been indicated in certain inscriptions discovered at an old site called Boghazkoi in Mesopotamia by the German archaeologist Hugo Winckler in 1907, and dated to about 1400 B.C. They record treaties between the kings of the Mitani and the Hittites. These were guaranteed by their gods called Mi-it-ra, U-ru-w-na, In-da-ra and Na-sa-at-ti-ia, corresponding to the Rigvedic Deities known as Mitra, Varuna, Indra and Nasatyas (the twin Asvins). Thus it has been assumed that Rigvedic Civilization was an established fact in India before 1400 B.C. so as to promote colonial, cultural and commercial activities up to a distant country like Mesopotamia. There are also other linguistic proofs of the spread of Indian civilization towards that remote region. The letters from Tel-el-Amarna mention Mitani princes bearing Sanskrit names like Artatama, Tusratta and Suttarna, while the gods of another people of that age, the Kassites (*c.* 1746-1180 B.C.), have names like Shurias (Sanskrit Surya) and Marytas (Marutas).

The same antiquity of Vedic civilization is pointed to by the fact that Buddhism which arose about 600 B.C. had its origin in Vedic thought as represented in the four types of literature known as the *Sutras, Aranyakas, Upanishads*, and the Vedic *Samhitas* originating from the *Rigveda* as the primary work. All this literary and linguistic development required sufficient time which Winternitz estimates at about

2000 years from 600 B.C. so as to render Vedic civilization at least as old as 2500 B.C.

The next landmark in the history of Indian expansion is found in the two practically contemporary documents, Panini's grammar (called *Ashtadhyayi*) and the inscriptions of the Achaemenian emperors of Persia. Macdonell has assigned to Panini 500 B.C. as his latest date, while R. G. Bhandarkar supposed it to be as old as about 750 B.C. The Achaemenian emperors of Persia who established connection with India were (1) Cyrus (558-530 B.C.) (2) Cambyses (530-522 B.C.) (3) Darius I (522-486 B.C.) and (4) Xerxes (486-465 B.C.) It was Cyrus who first annexed to the Persian empire a part of India which is called by Herodotus as Gandarites (Gandhara). In his earlier Behistan Inscription, Darius I also mentions Ga(n) dara as a part of his empire. But in his later inscriptions, he adds to it *Hi(n) dush* (*Sindhuh-Indus*) along with its other part called Gadara (=Gandhara). Darius in his earlier Behistan Inscription mentions as his subjects both *Yauna* (Ionians) and Gadara Xerxes recruited for his army his Indian subjects called Gandharians and Indians to fight in Greece, as stated by Greek writers.*

These Persian contacts brought to India both Persian script and coins, Gold (*Daric*) and Silver (*Sigloi*). That is why Panini, as a native of Gandhara, was acquainted with this foreign Persian script which he calls by the generic name of Yavanani explained by him as the script of the Yavanas *(Yavananam lipi)*. It was the Aramaic Script "which

* The Naqsh-i-rustam Inscription of Daraya-va(h)-ush (Darius I) mentions as parts of his empire (1) Ga(n)-dara and (2) Hi(n) dush (=Sindhuh). His Persepolis Inscription and that of his successor Khshuyarsha (=Xerxes) also repeat these two regions as parts of the empire. The Susa Palace Inscription mentions Hi(n) dauv (=Sindhau=Sindhoh) from which the Indian ivory was imported. The Hamadan Tablet inscription of Darius I also names *Hi(n) dauv* as a part of the Persian empire. But the earlier big palace Inscription of Susa mentions *Teak* imported from Ga(n) dara but omits mention of Sindhu.

was introduced into India in the sixth century B.C. when the north-west was under Persian rule, and when Aramaic was used as a means of communication for the purposes of government throughout the Persian Empire . . . Buhler rightly conjectured in 1895 that originally the Aramaic language and alphabet was imported into Gandhara" (Rapson in *CHI*, I, 62). Asoka, accordingly, used this Aramaic script for his inscription at Taxila for the benefit of his Yona (foreign) colony. It was not the colony of a remote people like the Ionians but of Iranians nearer home. The Aramaic Script produced the famous variety known as the Kharosthi Script which came to be used for the countries in North-Western India. Asoka mentions in his Rock Edicts V and XIII, the Yonas, Kambojas and Gandharas together as *Aparantas* or peoples on his frontiers. These frontier Yonas are to be distinguished from the subjects of the five *Yona-rajas* or Greek Kings mentioned in RE II and XIII. They were Antas or neighbours, and not borderers or *Aparantas.* The former were independent and outside of the limits of the empire. Again, Asoka calls his Governor Tushaspha as a *Yavana-raja*, an Iranian, and not an Ionian Chief. The *Vishnupurana* describes the Yavanas, and Kambojas by their repugnant social customs, eating beef, shaving head, and keeping beard, for which the Greeks were not known. The *Markandeya Purana* (Ch. 57) locates the *Yavanas* to the West (*paschime yavanah smritah*). The foreign peoples of the West were known by the generic term *Yavana* in Sanskrit. Again, in the old Buddhist canonical text of *Majjhima Nikaya* of about 5th century B.C. there is a reference (II. 149) to Yona and Kamboja society and to other peoples of the frontier regions (*annesucha pachchantimesu janapadesu*) which knew only of two social divisions (*dveva vanna*) instead of four, viz. the class of employers (*ayyo=arya*) and employed (*dasocha*).

India next achieved a remarkable expansion under the Maurya king, Chandragupta, who repelled the Greek invasion of Seleukos in *c.* 304 B.C. and annexed to his Indian empire the eastern part of the Syrian empire comprising the provinces of Gedrosia, Arachosia (Kandahar), Aria (Herat), and Paropamsidae (Hindukush), so that he came to rule over a Greater India which extended up to the borders of Persia. Accordingly, his grandson Asoka calls the King of Syria Antiochus (Amtiyoka) as his immediate neighbour (*Anta*) in his Rock Edict II. As a result of increased intercourse between India and Iran, there sprang up a large foreign settlement in the capital of India at Pataliputra, of which the Municipality had to constitute a special committee to take charge of its interests, as reported by the Greek Ambassador Megasthenes, deputed to the Mauryan Court. This Indian intercourse with Persia led Asoka to recruit, as a friendly gesture, for his office of the Governor of the Saurashtra Province, the Yona Chief, Raja Tushaspha (a Persian name), in succession to the Indian Governor, Pushyagupta Vaisya, under Chandragugpta.

India's foreign influence was very much increased and extended under Asoka who regularly organized pacific missions, medical and cultural, for work in foreign countries for humanitarian programmes like treatment of diseases (*Chikitsa*) and also preaching the gospel of Peace and Non-violence, the gospel of *Dharma-Vijaya*, the conquest of Truth, a conquest not of coercion, or violence, but of love (*Priti*) (RE. XIII).

At the same time, according to literary evidence, foreign missions were despatched by a Buddhist Council (*Sangiti*) which met under Asoka in the 17th year of his reign (c. 253 B.C.) in the royal monastery at Pataliputra in a nine months' session under an old Thera, Moggaliputta Tissa (who was conveyed to the capital comfortably in a ship on the Ganges and not in a jostling wheeled vehicle). Among the foreign countries to which these *theras* were sent as Missionaries to teach the doctrine suited to each are mentioned (1) Yavana (Western Country) (*Yonarattham*) (2) Suvarnabhumi (Pegu and Moulmein in Burma) and (3) Lanka (or Ceylon called Tamraparni in RE. II) whereto was despatched the Crown-Prince Mahendra. One of these Missionaries was a Yonaka named Dharmarakkhita, a Western Hindu, who was deputed to the Aparanta mentioned in R.E. VI and XIII as the land inhabited by the Yonas and Kambojas. Special attention was paid to the Himavanta-pradesa where five eminent Missionaries headed by Majjhima were sent to preach the most important doctrines of Buddhism as contained in the *Dharma-Chakra-Pravartana-Sutra*. They included such famous preachers as Kasapagota and Dadabhisara whose names are also mentioned in inscriptions on relic-caskets at Sanchi, besides Majjhima. Thus the truth of the legends is confirmed by Inscriptions.

The remarkable fact of Asoka's foreign missions is that by unprecedented self-sacrifice he deputed as permanent exiles his eldest son, Mahendra, and eldest daughter Samghamitra to work for the spread of Buddhism in the distant island of Ceylon. They were prepared for this religious mission by being duly ordained beforehand, Mahendra at the age of 20, in the 6th year of Asoka's reign (in 264 B.C.), and his sister at 18. Mahendra took 3 years as a monk to master the three *Pitakas* under Moggali as his Upadhyaya, while his sister was educated for the mission by Directress Dharmapala and the teacher Ayapala, (V. 204-210, *Mahav*.I. As pointed out by Vincent Smith, considering the close cultural relations thus established between India and Ceylon (Tamprapami), we must credit Asoka with a sea-going fleet as the instrument by which these relations could be maintained in these early days.

Lastly, we must note a most interesting fact attesting the extension of India's influence towards the West in certain countries of Europe. Asoka himself states in his Rock Edict XIII that his pacific missions, medical and cultural, were despatched by him to the five select countries of Europe then under the following Kings as his friends: (1) Amtiyoka

Yona-raja (=Antiochus Theos II of Syria) (261-246 B.C.), (2) Turamaye (=Ptolemy II Philadelphos of Egypt) (285-245 B.C.), (3) Amtikini (=Antigonus Gonatas of Macedonia) (278-239 B.C.), (4) Maka (=Magas of Cyrene) (West of Egypt) (300-258 B.C.) and (5) Alikasudara (=Alexander of Epirus) (272-258 B.C.). In all these neighbouring States (*Saveshu cha amteshu*), and also within his empire (*iha cha*), was being won (*ladho*) his proposed *Dharma-Vijaya*, Moral Conquest, with their peoples following his consequential religious injunctions (*Dhramanusasti Anuvatamti*).

As regards the Medical Missions, Asoka states in his Rock Edict II that both within his own dominion (*Vijite*) and in the States on his borders (*prachamtesu*) both in and out of India, the States of the Cholas and Pandyas, Satyaputras, and Keralaputras, and as far South as Tambapamni (Tamraparni), and also in the States of the neighbouring King Amtiyoka, and the States of his neighbours (*Samipam* or *Samanta rajano*) up to a distance of 600 yojanas, everywhere (*Sarvatra*), he has instituted (*Kata=Krita*) measures of medical treatment (*chikitsa*) of both men and animals (*Manusa-pasu-chikitsa*), with provision of medicines (*Osadhani*) and their sources in the roots (*mula*) and fruits (*phala*) of medicinal plants imported (*harapita*) from abroad or grown (*ropapita*) in the country.

The next important evidence of India's expansion overseas is furnished about six centuries after Asoka in the famous Allahabad Pillar Inscription of Emperor Samudragupta. It states how the peoples inhabiting Simhala and all other islands "overseas" (constituting what has been aptly called *Dvipantara-Bharata*) (*Samhalaka-dibhischa sarva-dvipavasibhih*) acknowledged the suzerainty of Samudragupta by rendering to him all kinds of service (*Seva*) comprising (1) *Atma nivedanam* (offering their persons at the service of the Emperor), (2) *Kanyo-payana* (gifts of maidens), (3) *Dana* (gifts) and (4) Application (*yachana*) for Charters bearing the imperial Gupta Garuda Seal (*Garutmadanka*) which would assure them the possession (*Bhukti*) and government (*Sasana*) of their respective territories (*Svavishaya*). They thus entered into treaties of Alliance and Service by which they were protected against aggression by 'an all-powerful emperor who brought the whole of India under his sway by the prowess of his arms' (*bahuvirya prasara-dharani bandhasya*).

The inclusion of Ceylon in Samudragupta's imperial system and sphere of influence is further proved by literary evidence. According to the Chinese author, Wang Hiuen-tse, a King of Ceylon named, Chi-mi-Kia-po-mo (=Sri Megha-Varman or Varna whose time was A.D. 350-380) cultivated cordial relations with Samudragupta to whom he sent an embassy with gifts for a proposal that he be permitted to construct at Bodh-Gaya a Monastery for the residence of Ceylonese pilgrims to that holy place.

CHAPTER IV

FOREIGN TRADE

THERE is some evidence to show that India from very early times carried on trade by sea with several foreign countries. According to Dr. Sayce, the Assyriologist, Indian teak has been found among the ruins of Ur about 3000 B.C. while Sindhu or Indian muslin is mentioned in an old Babylonian list of clothes. This Sindhu or muslin, as pointed out by Hewitt, was brought to Babylon by sea and not by land by Zend-speaking traders who would have called it by the Zend term Hindu. A beam of Indian cedar has been found in the palace of Nebuchadnezzar (604-562 B.C.) and also Indian teak at a temple of Ur. The old Baveru-Jataka (*c.* Sixth Century B.C.) tells of import by sea to Babylon of the Indian peacock. As Buhler states: "This trade very probably existed in much earlier times, as the *Jatakas* tell of other voyages and mention old ports like Surparaka (Sopara) and Bharukachchha (Broach)." The Buddhist canonical work *Digha-Nikaya* (*c* 5th Century B.C.) tells of ocean-going ships out of sight of land. India also exported to Babylon rice and sandal-wood which were known to the Greeks by their Indian names before 5th Century B.C. Thus "the evidence warrants us in the belief that maritime commerce between India and Babylon flourished in the sixth and seventh Century B.C." (Kennedy). A. M. T. Jackson states that "the Buddhist *Jatakas* and some of the Sanskrit law books tell us that ships from Broach and Sopara traded with Babylon from the 8th to the 6th Century B.C.

A vessel of Pharaoh brought to Egypt from India her products like "elephants' teeth, gold, precious stones, sandal-wood and monkeys." According to Wilkinson, the tombs of Egypt have brought to light Indian products like "Indigo, Tamarind-Wood," while, according to Lassen, "the Egyptians dyed cloth with Indigo and wrapped their mummies in Indian muslin."

The *Bible* also refers to some imports from India like precious stones in the Mosaic period (1491-1450 B.C.) and "ivory, garments, armour, spices and peacocks" in the days of Solomon (*c.* 1015 B.C.). The thesis is thus summed up by Rev. T. Faulkes (*IA*, Vol. VIII): "The fact is now scarcely to be doubted that the rich oriental merchandise of the days of King Hiram and King Solomon had its starting place in the sea-ports of the Dakhan, which also exported to Egypt some of its esteemed spices."

Lastly, it may be noted that specimens of Indian ivory, ape and peacock are on view at the Tutan Khanem Collection of the Cairo Museum and these I personally saw. Some of these exports from India like Peacock, Rice, Ginger, or Cinnamon were known in the West by their Tamil terms, e.g. Hebrew Biblical term *tuki* for peacock which corresponds to Tamil *Tokei*, as pointed out by Caldwell (*Comparative Grammar of Dravidian Languages*). He also says that the works of Pliny, Ptolemy and *Periplus* contain the largest stock of primitive Dravidian words.

This early Indian trade which began like a trickle grew into a substantial volume by the first three centuries of the Christian era during which was developed a profitable sea-borne trade between India and the West represented mainly by the Roman empire which became her best customer. This Roman trade is testified to both by literary texts and the more concrete and convincing evidence of abundant finds of Roman coins as the tangible results of that trade at several places in the South, specially at Coimbatore and Madura, as the chief centres of this export trade. It was Southern India which had the monopoly of the products which were in great demand in the West. There was a demand in the West for its botanical products like Pepper, Betel, Spices, and Scents; for the precious stones of her mines like Beryl, Gem, Diamond, Ruby and Amethyst; the pearls of her seas; the ivory from the tusks of her elephants; and the silks and muslins turned out by her handicrafts. "Roman beauties, decked in even seven folds of Muslin, and parading themselves on the highways of Rome, became a menace to its morals," till its import was banned by Roman Parliament. The test of this Indian muslin was that 20 yds. of it could be passed through a finger-ring.

Drain of Roman gold. The result of this foreign trade to India was the drain of Roman gold into India to pay for her imports which far exceeded her exports. Pliny (*Natural History*) estimates this drain at 100 million sesterces (=£1,000,000) per annum. It gave to India a favourable balance of trade. and a stable gold currency for the Kushana empire of those days.

Roman Settlements. There were also other consequences of this Roman trade to India's economy and politics. A Tamil work refers to settlements of *Yavana* (Roman) traders importing from Rome "wine, brass, lead, lamps and vases." A Tamil poem describes how a Tamil King "daily drank of his golden cups fragrant wine brought by the Yavanas in their good ships." A Tamil poet describes the thriving port of Muchiris at the mouth of the Periyar, "with the beautiful large ships of the Yavanas bringing gold and returning laden with Pepper. The gold was received from the ships in exchange for the articles sold and brought to shore in barges."

Employment of Roman Soldiers. Roman soldiery described as "powerful Yavanas of terrifying looks, and wearing long coats" were employed by the Tamil Kings to "guard their tents on battle-field." They are also described as "dumb Mlechchhas," because they could not speak with the people in their language but could only speak to them by gestures. Under a Pandya King, these foreign Roman soldiers were employed to guard the gates of Madura. Roman cohorts were also posted in garrisons set up at the port-towns like Muziris (Cranganore).

Kaveripattinam—a centre of foreign trade. At Kaveripattinam on the beach were constructed raised platforms, godowns, and warehouses for storing up goods landed from ships. The goods were first stamped with the Chola Tiger emblem after payments of customs duty, and then passed on to merchants' warehouses (*Pattinappalai*). Close by were "settlements of Yavana merchants, and quarters of foreign traders speaking various tongues." They were served by a big bazar where were available all things needed. There were "vendors of fragrant pastes and powders, of flowers and incense; tailors who worked on silk, wool or cotton; traders in sandal, coral, pearl, gold and precious stones; grain merchants; washermen; dealers in fish and salts; butchers; blacksmiths, braziers, carpenters, coppersmiths, goldsmiths; painters, sculptors, cobblers, and toy-makers. There were also horses brought to the market from distant lands beyond the seas."

Most of these goods were gathered for export. According to Pliny, India's exports included pepper and ginger which fetched a price of 100 times their original value. There was also a demand for the incenses, spices and aromatics of India. It was due to the lavish consumption of these commodities at Rome at religious and funeral ceremonies. Nero burnt at a funeral a year's produce of cinnamon and cassia. At the funeral of Scylla, 210 loads of spices were strewn upon the pyre.

The interests of these foreign colonies were protected by diplomatic agreements negotiated by embassies. A Pandya king sent an embassy to the Roman Emperor Augustus of the 1st Century B.C. Embassies were also sent to Trojan after 99 A.D.

Ports. This brisk trade flowed through ports located on both the Malabar and Coromandal Coasts. These are described in Roman works like those of Pliny and Ptolemy and especially in the Greek work, *Periplus*, of 1st Century A.D. On the West Coast sprang up ports like "Sopara (Sopara), Barygaza (Broach), Kalliena (Kalyana) and Muziris (Cranganore), while the Coromandal coast had also its string of ports through which was carried on the trade with "Golden Chersonese (Suvarnabhumi) and Golden Chyrse (Suvarnadvipa)." The ports under the Cholas were equipped with "lighthouses, exhibiting blazing lights at night to guide ships to ports," as stated in the Tamil text.

A very interesting piece of evidence has been unearthed at a site called Arekamedu near Pondicherry in specimens of the famous Italian pottery known as *Arretine*, with the Italian potter's stamps imprinted on them, such as *Vibie* (of first century B.C.) and *Gaius* (of the Claudian period, 41-54 A.D.). Along with this foreign pottery was also found the fragment of a Roman lamp.

There is some evidence of foreign trade in the Andhra empire of the times. Some of its ports and inland towns took part in this trade. Thus the town of Paithana (Pratishthana) shipped abroad its onyx stones, and Tagara, its cottons, muslins and other textiles. The Andhra king Yajnasri issued a rare type of coins figuring the ship as the symbol of the State's sea-borne trade.

CHAPTER V

INDUSTRIAL ACHIEVEMENT

EARLY Indian economy was natuially a village economy which persists predominantly to this day. The reason is that India still continues as an agricultural country comprising about 5 lakhs of villages as against only a few towns, numbering only about forty of 1 lakh population or over each. It is thus a rural and not an urban civilization. About 80% of its population still live on land with an average holding of about 1½ acres of land per head and 3 acres for a family of five. These agricultural millions have to find their support by cultivation of land only for about half the year. The other half is the off-season of agriculture, during which they must find other means of livelihood, mostly by handicrafts, and partially by transport and small trade.

Thus the old Indian rural economy had to base itself upon a balanced development of agriculture and industry. It was, however, able to render a good account of industrial progress within the limits of a restricted economy.

Perhaps the earliest Mining industry of the world was founded in India. As is already stated, in the Indus Valley city of Mohenjo-Daro of *c*. 3000 B.C. women used a variety of ornaments of gold, of which the only source in those early days was the Kolar Gold fields of Mysore State. This conclusion has been reached by a committee of metallurgical experts headed by Sir Edwin Pascoe under the direction of Sir John Marshall. This Committee subjected this ancient gold of Mohenjo-Daro to a chemical analysis and found that it contained in its composition a proportion of Silver

Alloy, 11% electron, which is also found in the gold ores of the Kolar fields, and in no other known source. This discovery thus throws light upon both cultural and economic history. Not only was gold-mining an early Indian industry. The precious products of the remote South found their market in the North. The North and South were not isolated by the natural barriers of the Vindhya hills or the impenetrable wilderness of Dandakaranya but were bound together in ties of close commercial and cultural intercourse which ultimately spread Aryan thought throughout India up to its limits, overcoming all its physical barriers.

There is also evidence of other mining projects in that early age. The entire Indus civilization was the product of material which was not locally available but had to be gathered from places far and near in and out of India. This Chalcolithic civilization depended most on copper. The copper used in it contained in its composition proportions of Arsenic and Nickel which marked the variety then obtained only from the Rajasthan mines. The tin used is traceable to casserite then found in what is now the State of Bombay, parts of Bihar and Orissa, and chiefly in the mines of Hazaribagh. Tin was not used by itself but as an alloy with copper so as to form *Bronze* containing 6 to 13% of tin.

Besides Metals and Minerals, this old civilization was also built on Stone of different kinds. It was quarried at different sites. Lime-stone used for covering drains was quarried at Sukkur. Gypsum used as mortar came from quarries of Kirthar hills far away. The beautiful yellow stone was quarried in Jaisalmer. Other mines in Rajasthan yielded steatite and slate. Amethyst was derived from the Deccan trap. Then there was the singular and beautiful Green Amazon Stone of which the nearest quarry was in the far South, a place known as Doddabetta in the Nilgiris. The green stone for its beauty was in request even in remote Mesopotamia. Sir Leonard Woolley in charge of archaeological excavations at the old city of Ur found in one of its early layers "two beads of Amazonite, a green stone, for which the nearest source is in the Nilgiri Hills, calling up the astonishing picture of antideluvian man engaged in a commerce which sent its caravans across a thousand miles of mountain and desert from the Mesopotamian Valley into the heart of India."

The remains of the civilization also testify to the industry of spinning carried out by spindle whorls of faience, pottery and shell, while cotton was also cultivated probably for the first time in the world.

It also produced glazed pottery, "the earliest example of its kind in the ancient world."

There was also some progress in artistic craftsmanship. On its seals were carved life-like figures of animals like the humped bull, buffalo, bison, tiger, lion, elephant, horse and ram.

Figures were executed in stone of a Yogi with his eyes fixed in meditation upon the tip of the nose, or of a dancing girl in bronze.

We have already described the remarkable degree of success achieved by India in the early centuries of the Christian era in the production of fine silks and muslins for which there was a great rage in Rome. These exports helped to create a favourable balance of trade by the drain of gold out of Rome into India to pay for her imports, as described by Mommsen.

We may now refer to some of the outstanding examples of industrial achievement in the course of India's history.

Mauryan history of the third and second century B.C. in the times of Chandragupta and Asoka is marked by several monumental works. It gave to India its first dam and reservoir, aptly called Beautiful or *Sudarsana* in a later inscription of King Rudradaman I of 150 A.D. It describes how a *Tataka* or lake was created by damming up the flow of rivers such as "Suvarnasikata, Palasini and others," down the hills then called Raivataka and Urjayat, under Emperor Chandragupta and his Governor (*Rashtriya*) of Surashtra. Under Asoka and his Governor, the Yona chief, Raja Tushaspha, the lake was equipped with supplemental channels (*pranali*) for distribution of the water impounded in the reservoir for irrigation in the down country. This reservoir was a piece of most eduring construction. It was vast like an ocean (*sambhonidhitulya*), and lasted for more than seven centuries after Asoka, up to the time of the Gupta emperor Skanda Gupta. In his reign, in the year 455 A.D. "at the advent of the monsoons" (*ambudakala agate*) piercing the heat of summer season (*nidagha kalam pravidarya*), there occurred a continuous downpour of rain (*vavarsha toyam*) by which the dam suddenly (*afvarat*) burst (*bibheda*), so as to release the imprisoned streams (*chirabandhana ushitah*) which at once found their way into the sea (*samudra-krantah*), and rendered the beautiful lake an ugly-looking (*durdarsana*) one." The breach, however, was repaired and the embankment renewed within the short period of two months with a length of 100 cubits, width of 68, and height of 7 men, as a solid work of masonry (*samyak-ghatita-upalena*) so as to last for all time (*Sasvata-kalpa-kalam*). The then Governor of Saurashtra-*Avani* was Pahlava Suvisakha whose rare patriotism and civic spirit led him to pay the entire colossal expenditure incurred (*dhanasya kritva vyayam aprameyam*) on the repair of Sudarsana lake (*Sudarsana tataka samskara*) out of his privy purse (*svasmat koshat*), instead of charging it to public funds (Junagarh inscription of Skanda Gupta. No. 1, of Fleet).

Mauryan India also achieved success in other fields of Engineering, in Town-planning, Architecture, and Art. An example of town-planning was its capital itself, Pataliputra, which was founded at a strategic site at the confluence of the two rivers, Ganga and Sona. It was constructed as a city, with a length of 9 miles, and width of 1, and protected by a moat 60 feet deep and 200 yards wide, and the further defence of a massive timber palisade pierced by loopholes, through which archers could shoot. The palisade was provided with 64 openings or gates and 570 towers, as reported by an eye-witness, the Greek Ambassador Megasthenes, who came to live in that city. The city had also its palace worthy of it in its magnificence, with its extensive park of groves and evergreen trees attracting all kinds of birds, peacocks, pheasants and parrots flocking round the king and large tanks breeding the biggest fish. The interior of the palace was adorned with gilded pillars clasped by vines embossed in gold, and decorated with birds of silver. The sewage of the city found its outlet in the rivers.

Asoka made his own contributions to the improvement of the palace by replacing its wooden material by stone which was so lavishly utilised by him in constructing his other monuments. It stood out through centuries in all its pristine magnificence which was even seen in all its splendour more than six centuries later by the Chinese pilgrim, Fa-hien, who visited India under Emperor Chandra Gupta II. He thus reports on what he still saw of it: "The royal palace and halls in the midst of the city, which exist now as of old, were all made by spirits which he employed, and which piled up the stones, reared the walls and gates, and executed the elegant carving and inlaid sculpture work in a way which no human hand of this world could accomplish." This statement of a learned foreign observer constitutes the highest compliment that can be paid to the degree of perfection achieved by Mauryan Engineering in the field of Art and Architecture, and described as superhuman by an impartial eye-witness from another great country with similar achievements to its credit.

The Asokan Pillar stands out as another noteworthy example of ancient Indian Art and Architecture. It is noted as much for its original and appropriate design as for its successful execution. The Pillar was designed as a monolithic shaft with a foundation of 12 feet, tapering up to an average height of 50 feet, crowned by a capital to serve as a religious symbol. For Asokan Art was at the service of his religious mission and not an appeal to the senses. The religious significance of the Pillar informs all its parts. At the foundation is found the figure of a peacock (*mayura*) as the symbol of the Moriya Dynasty. The trunk of the Pillar was made to convey through the centuries in a permanent form the royal religious message of Morality inscribed on it in indelible characters. Every inch of the Pillar and its valuable space is utilized for the highest purpose of mass-education in morals. The culmination is reached at the top or capital made up of three parts comprising (1) a big wheel placed on the shoulders of (2) four lions set back to back and (3) abacus decorated by figures of four animals with a smaller wheel alternating between them. The four animals, the elephant, bull, horse, and lion are symbolical of the four turning-points of the Master's life from Nativity to Buddhahood, while the wheel is the *Dharma-Chakra* (Kingdom of Righteousness) which was inaugurated by him at Sarnath, the place of the pillar marking out that great event of the Buddha's first preaching. The big wheel on Lions is designed as one of 32 spokes, the thirty-two marks of the Superman (*Mahapurusha-lakshanam*). Thus every part and detail of the Pillar is a religious symbol.

The Asokan Pillar is also conspicuous for its polish which is "the despair of modern masons", as stated by Vincent Smith. The polish was so bright and blazing that both Tom Coryat and Whittekar (Kerr's *Voyages and Travels,* IX 423) coolly described it as a pillar of brass, Chaplain Terry as a pillar of marble, and Bishop Heber as a pillar of "Cast-metal." It is also possessed of features testifying to the skill attained in the art of dressing, chiselling, and shaping stone.

It also poses a problem of transport. In the first place, its material was quarried in the hills of Chunar whence it was carried to the central workshop at the capital of Pataliputra where it was shaped after a uniform design so as to have the average height of 50 feet and weight of 50 tons. Secondly, these gigantic pillars and heavy weights had to be moved to their appointed sites like Meerut at a distance of more than 1000 miles from their place of fabrication. The location of the Pillar thus presented a formidable problem of transport. It was tackled by Sultan Feroz Shah Taghlak who took it into his head to decorate the city of Delhi by planting in it the Asokan Pillar which he saw at Topra near Ambala. Its removal from such a short distance to Delhi called for the making of a special cart of 42 wheels at each of which pulled 200 men. The labour-force of 8400 men was required for the haulage of the Pillar and its transport in different stages to its destination. According to another account, elephants were first tried to draw the cart and then 20,000 men.

Lastly, a reference may be made in this connection to some of the metallurgical marvels produced in ancient India. One of these is the Iron Pillar at Kutab in Delhi made of material which is pure, rustless, malleable iron, a standing monument which has defied for more than a millennium the ravages of time, the wear and tear of weather and the attack of oxidation. Its composition was examined by a Committee of Experts who have held that it was beyond the capacity of any Iron Foundry of that age (*c.* 400 A.D.) to produce such a finished metallurgical masterpiece. India also produced the steel of which was made the famous Damascus blade. The *Brihatsamhita* of Varahamihira mentions a particular preparation of cement which is described as *Vajralepa*, 'cement strong like the thunderbolt'. It was this enduring cement which must have gone into the making and strengthening of the joints of the Asokan Pillar which still stands four-square to the winds through more than 20 centuries at Nandangarh where it braved the earthquake of 1934, which laid low the palaces of kings and razed to the ground many a solidly-built city.

Another metallurgical masterpiece of ancient India is the Sultangang colossal image of the Buddha in copper. "It is made of very pure copper, cast in two dagers over an inner core by a sort of *circ perdu* process. It is 7½ feet high and weighs about a ton. A people which was capable of producing such works in stone and iron must have attained considerable proficiency in metallurgy and engineering" [p. 338 of *Legacy of India,* (Oxford)].

CHAPTER VI

DEMOCRATIC TRADITIONS

THE *Rigveda* which is the earliest work of mankind contains the earliest conception of democracy and gives expression to it in appropriate institutions called *Sabha* and Samiti. It is so committed to democratic ideals that it has made of Democracy a Deity aptly called *Samjnana* or *Samajuana* to whom its last hymn (Sukta) is addressed. The term *Samjnana* denotes the collective consciousness of the people, the National Mind to which the individual mind is to pay its homage as the source from which it derives its potency. The hymn calls upon the people to gather in their Assembly (*samgachchhaddhvam*) and speak there in one voice (*samvadaddhvam*) in a union of minds (*sammanah*), of heart (*samachittam*), of policy (*samana-mantrah*), and of hopes and aspirations (*akuti*). Thus democracy depends upon the inner unity of its citizens, their emotional integration.

The democratic principle was at work in the different spheres of public life, political, social, and cultural. Social life was organised in a hierarchy of institutions such as (1) *Griha* or *Kula*, (2) *Grama*, (3) *Vis*, the canton or clan and (4) *Jana* or the people or *Samsad* organised into *Rashtra* or State.

In the cultural sphere, there were *Samghas* of learned men who by their discussions evolved out of popular speech (*vacham laukikim*) the refined Sanskrit "like groats through a sieve." Education was also promoted by learned conferences meeting at the courts of kings. The Upanishads tell of the Philosophical Congress which was convened by

Janaka, king of Videha, and helped by its discussions to codify Hindu Philosophy under the leadership of Rishi Yajnavalkya. Eight philosophers as exponents of different schools of thought participated in these discussions along with a woman-philosopher named Gargi.

Monarchy was the normal form of Vedic polity but it was a limited constitutional monarchy. The theory was that Dharma or Law was the real sovereign, while the king or the Executive was the *Danda* to uphold and enforce it. Thus the autocracy of the Vedic king was limited by democratic checks such as his election and expulsion. Vedic democracy also knew of the vote of the majority for which the term used is *Narishta* which Sayana explains as "inviolable as the voice of the many" (*bahavah sambhuya yadi ekam vakyam vadeyuh tat hi na paraih atilanghyam*).

The Vedic democratic tradition governed the entire growth of Indian Polity through the ages. Even where it took on the form of a monarchy, it was a limited or constitutional monarchy, so that the pattern of polity remained fundamentally democratic. It was based on decentralisation and local autonomy. It believed in the self-government of the group. Scope was given to the natural associations and groupings of people in autonomous corporations providing for exercises in self-government which was necessary to revive the decaying social tissues. These corporations were formed in the following ascending order, viz.,

(1) *Kula* (clan or family)

(2) *Jati* (caste)

(3) *Sreni* (guild of followers of the same crafts)

(4) *Puga* (a larger body bringing together different castes and crafts—the village community) and

(5) *Janapada* (the entire region or State).

Each of these groups had its own laws within its sphere, which the king had to respect. Thus monarchy had to reconcile itself to a subterranean democracy operating in different strata and stages of self-government down to the village.

Side by side with the monarchy thus limited by popular rule, there also developed the regular republican type of polity of which glimpses are given in different literary texts, Brahminical, Buddhist and Jain.

Panini found in the working republics of his time terms to illustrate his grammatical rules. He finds the terms *Nikaya, Gana* and *Sangha* applied to different public bodies of his times. The *Nikaya* was a religious association which was worked as a democracy and did not recognise inequality of status, high or low (*Uttara-adhara*), among its members. In religion all are equal.

Gana and *Sangha* were the usual terms for a republic.

Gana was so called because its sovereignty vested in the many (*ganadhinah*) as contrasted with kingship or government by one (*Eka-raja=Ekadhinah*) (Katyayana, IV. 1, 168). Further, the *Gana* was ruled by a special governing caste of Kshatriyas known as *Rajanyas* (Panini, VI. 2, 34). It had to observe Quorum as indicated in the term *Ganatitha* (V. 2, 52), explained as *Ganasya puranam*, implying the whip of an Assembly. As regards the term *Sangha*, it was applied to both individual republics and their Unions. Among individual Republics are mentioned the Kshudraka, Malava and Yaudheya *Sanghas*. As examples of Republican Federations are mentioned the Andhaka-Vrishni *Sangha* or the Trigarta *Sangha* which was a League of six republics (V. 3, 114, 116).

The *Sangha* government was based upon the party system. A Party was called a *Varga* and named after its leader, like a Vasudeva-*Varga* or an Arjuna-*Varga* (IV. 3, 64). There was a rivalry for power between the parties by opposition (*dandva*, VI. 2, 34) or by competition (*vyutkramana*, VIII. 1, 157). Some *Sanghas* were military classes called *Ayudhajivi*; Sanghas who lived by the profession of arms (IV. 2,

45, V. 3, 117) and were mostly in the Panjab or Vahika country.

The Executive of a Federation was composed of *Rajanya* leader of each constituent republic, such as Akrura and Vasudeva, attending its meetings with their rival *Vargas*.

The *Sangha* transacted its business by the *Chhanda* or vote of its members (IV. 4, 93). Panini calls the spirit of loyalty to the State, *Bhakti* (IV. 3, 100). Thus the term *Angaka* denotes the citizen of *Anga* (*Angah Janapada bhaktirasya*).

The *Mahabharata* is also acquainted with republics called *Samghata-gana*. Republican Unions are also called *Sanghas*. The *Mahabharata* (XII. 81) mentions the five republican peoples, Andhakas, Vrishnis, Yadavas, Kukuras, and Bhojas as forming themselves into a *Sangha* or Federation under Krishna as the *Sangha-Mukhya* or Federal President. Each constituent republic had its own leader called *Isvara*. Thus the Bhojas including Baladeva had Akrura as their leader. The party system was vigorously at work. There was a keen struggle for power among the party leaders dominated by Krishna, with his loyal following of such powerful personalities as Ahuka, Akrura, Gada, Pradyumna, and Samkarshana Baladeva, while the Leader of Opposition to him was Babhru Ugrasena (XII. 81, 3040). The *Mahabharata* refers to the *Gana* being governed by its Council of Leaders called *Gana-mukhyas*.

The Jain and Buddhist texts refer to regular republics of those days. There was a large republican Confederation called *Vajji* (Vriji) made up of nine Mallakis, nine Lichchhavis, and 18 *Gana-rajyas* of the region of Kasi-Kosala (*attharasa vi Ganarayano*). The death of Mahavira was the occasion of a federal funeral illumination arranged by these 36 republics in honour of "the Light of Intelligence that was gone" (*Bhagavati Sutra*, 300). The leader of this Confederation was the Lichchhavi Chief, Chetaka, who was Mahavira's uncle.

The Lichchhavis were governed by a Council of 7707 Rajas who were the chiefs of its principal families known as *Raja-Kulas* (cf. *Vesali nagare Ganaraja Kulanam abhisheka-mangala-pokkharini* of the *Jataka*). The republican Executive was one of eight *Kulas* (*ashta-Kulaka*) in charge of Justice, and nine in charge of foreign affairs. The part that was played by these *Rajas* in the Republics is probably indicated by the term *Rajasabdopajivinah* used by Kautilya (XI. 1) for these Sanghas i.e. those that functioned as their Rajas or Governors. Kautilya (XI.1) states that in Kamboja and Surashtra, there were Srenis or Corporations of Kshatriyas and other castes, who lived by economic or military pursuits (*Varta-sastropa-jivinah*), while the communities like the Lichchhivika, Vrijika, Mallaka, and others earned their living as Rajas or administrators. They were like the aristocracies of Aristotle.

The Lichchhavis had to face the hostility of emperor Ajatasatru who crushed the republic by weakening its unity and superior military force.

The *Sakya* republic is famous for giving to the world the Buddha who was thus a born democrat. It consisted of 80,000 families, and had its Parliament or *Parishad* of 500 members under a President called *Raja*. Its new building was inaugurated by the Buddha by His discourses (*Majjhima*, I. 353f.).

The *Malla* State of Pava, also a *Sangha-rajya* (*Majjhima*, I. 231) had its new Parliament House called *Ubbhataka* formally opened by the Buddha (*Samgiti-Sukta*). It gave to Buddhism some of its greatest characters like Ananda and Aniruddha.

Among other Republics mentioned in the texts are:

(1) The Nayas or *Jnatrikas* of Vaisali who gave to the world the Great Mahavira whose father was their chief;

(2) The Koliyas;

(3) The Moriyas of Pipphalavana; and

(4) The Videhas of Mithila.

Alexander's invasion of the Panjab during 327-325 B.C. was resisted heroically by its republican communities lying on its way. Firstly, there were the Aspasioi (=Asvayana of Panini, IV, 1, 110), Assakenoi (=Asvakayana of Panini, IV. 1, 99) and Astakenoi (=Hastinayana of Panini near the confluence of the Swat with the Kabul, with their capital at Pushkalavati), who fought the foe to a man. A repeated resistance was offered to him by the eastern Asvakayanas led by their Queen Cleophis (Krishna) and their women (Panini, IV. 285). There was another centre of this republican resistance at the fortress of Aornos (=Varana of Panini, IV. 282). Next, resistance came from the Glaussai (=Sans. Glauchukayanaka), the Adraistoi (Adhrishtas), and the Kathaoi (Kathas). Opposition was also organised by a confederacy of republican peoples led by the Malloi (Malavas) and the Oxydrakai (Kshudrakas). They had a city of Brahmanas who left the pen for the sword and died fighting for freedom. Other resisting republican peoples were the Sivis (Sibae), Abastanes (Ambashthas of Panini, IV. 1, 74), the Xathri (Kshatriyas), the Ossadioi (=Vasati of Panini, IV, 2, 53) and the Sogdi (Sudras).

Thus the democratic tradition was continuing strong through the ages. The Pali texts throw light upon the practices and procedure which kept it up, and anticipated their modern equivalents. For instance, the Sangha or Assembly had its Speaker called *Vinayadhara*, Whip called *Ganapuraka*, Resolution *Jnapti*, Vote *Chhanda*, and Decision by Vote of the majority, *Bhuyasika Kriya*. An incomplete Assembly (*Sangha*) lacking Quorum was called Vyagra, while the complete body was called *Samagra*. The Act (*Vaggakamma*) of an incomplete chapter of Bhikshus was considered invalid (*akammam*) and should not be transacted (*nakaraniyam*).

Notice (*Jnapti*) had first to be given of the Resolution to be moved (*sthapanam*). It was duly announced (*anussavanam*) and passed by three repeated readings (cf. *tini Kammavachahi kammam karoti-tritiyamapi etad artham vadami*) as a *Jnapti-chaturtha-karma*. Silence at each reading was taken as the Sangha's consent (*Kshamati Sanghasya-tasmat tushnim-evam etam dharayamiti*). But a Resolution also gave rise to debate, dispute (*Vivada*), quarrel (*Kalaha*) and even violence (*Chandana*) and "pointless" (*anagra*) speeches. To avoid a split in the *Sangha* (*Sangha-bheda*), a committee of the leaders of each contesting group was set up to reach unanimous decision which was then binding on the general parent body. But if it was not possible, then, as a last resort, recourse was taken to voting and decision by vote of the majority (*Yebbhuyyasikena*). Thus unanimity was the objective to be achieved by all means by solving the differences of minority and majority through the sub-committee of Arbitrators aptly called the *Udvahika Sabha*, "the committee to carry over to a decision." Vote was called *Chhanda* as used by Panini. It had to be taken by a Polling Officer who should be above prejudice, malice (*dosa*), folly (*moha*) and fear (*bhaya*) and appointed by a special Resolution of the *Samgha*. Voting was by Tickets (*salaka*) consisting of slips of wood of different colours to represent different opinions. Each member was to choose a ticket of the colour corresponding to his views, and to keep it a secret. The Polling Officer was called *Salaka grahapaka*.

CHAPTER VII

BUDDHIST COUNCILS

THE Buddhist Councils are examples of the application of the democratic principle in the sphere of religion. These are described in the *Mahavamsa*.

The first council was convened under the following circumstances. The sage Mahakassapa was travelling with his disciples from Pava to Kasinara, and on the way, hears of the death of the Buddha, whereupon the monks are deeply aggrieved. Subhadda cheaply consoles them by saying that they will now enjoy freedom from the Master's irksome control, and could now do what they would. This remark cut to the quick the devout Mahakassapa who at once resolved to combat the threatened licence of monks by undertaking a *Samgiti* or compilation of the *Dhamma* and *Vinaya*, so that the Doctrine may be kept pure. He also recalled that "the Sage had commanded the establishment of the Holy Truth, and a compilation of the Holy Dharma," and so he appointed to that end 500 eminent Bhikkhus. They met and decided that they should assemble and spend the coming rainy season at Rajagaha, and there make a compilation of the *Dhamma*. Its King, Ajatasattu, when informed that the monks would hold the Council (*Dhamma Samgiti*) in his city, fixed its place on Vebhara rock, on which with all speed he had a splendid Hall built at the entrance of the Sattapanni grotto, had precious mats spread in it for the seating of the monks, with a lofty seat for the *Thera* or President (*Therasana*), and a high seat in the middle for the Preacher (*Dhammasana*)." In a democratic manner, the Assembly of the Theras elected the Thera Upali to speak for the *Vinaya*, and

Ananda for the rest of the *Dhamma*. The great Thera Mahakassapa, sitting in the presidential chair, asked Upali questions touching the *Vinaya*, and Upali, seated in the preacher's chair, answered them, and expounded the matter. "And, as this best master of the *Vinaya* expounded each clause in turn, all the Bhikkus knowing the custom, repeated the *Vinaya* after him. The same procedure was followed in the case of Ananda as preacher of the *Dharma*." The *Sangiti* held its session for 7 months and completed the compilation of the Dhamma. Two facts are added to this account by *Chullavagga*. The first is that Ananda stated that the Buddha had permitted the *Sangha* to do away with 'the less important precepts'. But the Council, to avoid controversy, resolved not to do away with any precept. The second fact added is the entry of Purana into the Council to whom he said that he 'prefers to hold by that which he himself has heard from the Master's lips.'

Second Council. The Second Council called *Vinaya Samgiti* met 100 years after the *Parinirvana* of the Buddha, at Vaisali, though another tradition makes Pataliputra its meeting-place. It was called for by the mal-practices of the city-dwelling monks of Vesali, who showed alarming looseness of monastic discipline, while those who lived in the forests (*Aranyakah*) were more strict. The mal-practices of these urban monks were ten in number (*dasa vatthuni*). These included such practices as (1) going into a village after the meal, and there taking a second meal, if invited; (2) the carrying out of alleged official Acts, even if they are passed by an incomplete Chapter and hence invalid; or (3) accepting gold and silver as gifts (*Jataruparajatam*). At that time, in Vesali, many Bhikkhus of the Vajji confederacy shamelessly preached that these ten practices were lawful. At Vesali lived also a Thera named Yasa, a Brahmin, who was gifted with supernatural powers, such as 'the heavenly ear', 'the power to read the thoughts of others', 'the knowledge of previous lives' and 'freedom from all *asavas* or sins.' He was wandering about in the Vajji country, and betook himself to the Mahavana Vihara at Vesali where he resolved to settle this matter of the erring Bhikkhus. It so happened that in its Uposatha Hall, some of the monks placed a metallic vessel filled with water and began to ask the lay-visitors: "Bestow on the brotherhood *Kahapanas*" (Sans. Karshapana, a square copper coin weighing 146.4 grains= 9.48 grammes) and so on. The Thera, hearing these words, forbade the lay-folk with the words: "This is unlawful; give nothing!" These monks, thus frustrated and put to shame, then tried to assault the Thera who at once left the place for Kosambi, wherefrom he sent messengers to the Bhikkhus of Pava and Avanti, while he himself proceeded to Anoganga Mountain to relate all these happenings to the Thera Sambhuta Sanavasi residing there. They were joined here by 60 great Theras from Pava and 80 from Avanti, and, later, by an overwhelming number of monks from this and that region, who all tried to seek out their chief, the deeply learned Thera named Revata of Soreyya (near Takkasila). Revata by intuition sensed the situation, the crisis that was developing in the Church at Vesali which he reached soon and was received there by the Thera Yasa who at once questioned him on the Ten Points at dispute. These were rejected at once by Revata who said: "The heretical monks also tried to win him over by lawful gifts and sumptuous feeding." But the Thera did not accept them and dismissed his pupil, Uttara, who took these gifts from the sinful Vajjian monks. In the meantime, thousands of monks assembled under Revata at Vesali "to bring the dispute to a peaceful end." "And the Thera" (as a true democrat) could not end the dispute save in the presence of those with whom it began (*mulatthehi vina*, without those who were at the root). In the meanwhile, the then King of Magadha, under divine inspiration, set out from Pataliputra to go to Vesali where he proceeded to the Mahavana Vihara, assembled the congregation of the Bhikkhus there, and hearing both sides on the points of dispute, did not agree with the dissenting monks, left the congregation with the mandate "Do what you think best to further the Doctrine," promising to be their protector.

Then the brotherhood formally met to decide upon the disputed points. But the decision was delayed by endless controversy and 'pointless speeches' (*anaggani bhassani*), whereupon Revata "resolved to settle the matter by means of an *Ubbahika*. He appointed four Bhikkus from the East and four from Pava for the *Ubbahika* to set the dispute to rest." These eight Theras then betook themselves to a quiet and solitary retreat called Balikarama where Revata took the lead in putting questions to the others who unanimously disapproved the unlawful practices of the erring Vajjian monks. And when the committee ended their task, they placed their decision before the whole brotherhood whose opinions were elicited by the same method of question and answer which did not leave any scope for ambiguity. These opinions went against the heretical Bhikkhus.

Next, Revata decided to hold a Council of 700 select Bhikkhus. They met in the Balikarama and compiled the Dharma (*akarum dhammasamgaham*). This work they completed in eight months.

The heretical Monks, however, held a separate Council called *Mahasamgiti* and made out a different redaction of the Canonical Scriptures, on the basis of which they formed themselves into a separate sect called *Mahasamghika* as the first schism of the Buddhist Church which was hitherto a unit called *Theravada*. But "afterwards arose other Schools of Doctrine" known as *Achariyavada*. Thus in the second century arose 17 Schools and other Schools arose afterwards." (MV, V).

We must not, however, exaggerate the significance of these schisms. We may recall the wise words attributed by Vasumitra to the Buddha about these: "These Schools will be repositories of the diversified fruits of my scriptures without priority or inferiority. Just as the taste of the sea-water is everywhere the same. so will be the exposition of my doctrine advocated by these Schools."

The Second Council, like the first, is designated *Vinaya-samgiti*. It contributed to the completion of the *Vinaya* and *Dhamma*.

Third Council. The third Buddhist Council was held in the 17th year of King Asoka, i.e. in about 253 B.C. under circumstances narrated by the *Mahavamsa* in its Chapter V. In the time of Asoka, the revenues of the Buddhist church greatly increased with the increase of converts. This wealth tempted the heretics to take the yellow robe and to live with the Bhikkhus. "They proclaimed their own doctrines as the Doctrine of the Buddha and carried out their own practices even as they wished." The Bhikkhus could not restrain them, as they were numerically strong and unruly. The result was great disorder among them, with their suspension of important ceremonies like *Uposatha*. On hearing this, Asoka sent his mandate to his own Monastery Asokarama that its monks must observe *Uposatha*. Its community of Monks replied: "We hold not the *Uposatha* festival with heretics." In the trouble that ensued, Asoka's Minister who conveyed that royal command killed some Theras. This upset Asoka who exclaimed: "Is there a Bhikkhu who is able to set my doubts to rest and to befriend religion?" The brethren at once recommended to him the Thera Tissa, son of Moggali. The king then sent for him with a large escort three times, but the Saint did not come till he was told of the mission "to befriend religion." The Thera was then brought down the Ganges by a ship to Pataliputra where he first taught the religion of the Sambuddha to Asoka who afterwards assembled in his *Arama* the entire community of monks among whom were found thousands of heretics who were expelled from the order. Out of the rest, the Thera chose 1,000 who were proficient in the three *Pitakas* and the four Special Sciences to make a compilation of the True Doctrine with his aid. "In the midst of this Council the Thera Tissa set forth the *Kathavathuppakaranakarana* refuting the other doctrines." The Council had a Session of 9 months.

Geiger points out that the Third Council completed in essentials the canonical literature of the *Dhamma* and *Vinaya*, as we now have it in Pali. This is proved by the Bhabru Edict of Asoka mentioning seven scriptures, of which six are found in the Pali canon. The *Abhidhamma* was also compiled at this time because Tissas' work *Kathavatthuppakarana* was a part of the *Abhidhamma*.

The Pataliputra Council is, however, of more importance to Buddhism by the steps it took to send out teachers to preach it in countries beyond the border of its narrower original home. It thus laid the beginnings of a Greater India in an expansion of Buddhism in eastern Asia including Indonesia. Thus the three Buddhist Councils built up the literature of Buddhism by the fruitful democratic method of discussion in learned Conferences giving scope to free and unfettered exposition of different views and doctrines out of which emerged its true tenets.

CHAPTER VIII

ASOKA THE GREAT
(c 274-235 B.C.)

ASOKA is a unique character in the annals of royalty and, indeed, as a man too. H. G. Wells considers him as the greatest of kings. He was great as the ruler of an extensive dominion (*mahalake hi vijite*) which was large like *prithivi*, as he himself describes it in his proclamations written on the rocks of ages (RE XIV and V). This far-flung empire which extended from Persia to Ceylon was his legacy from his grandfather Chandragupta who had acquired it by his conquests. One of these was the eastern part of the Syrian Empire under its king Seleukos who invaded India under Chandragupta in about 304 B.C. but was defeated and had to cede to the victor the provinces called Gedrosia (Baluchistan), Aria (Herat), Arachosia (Kandahar) and Paropamsidae (Hindukush). Thus Asoka as his successor came to rule over a Greater India which extended from Syria (Persia) to Tamraparni (Ceylon) and was able to call the Syrian king Antiochus II (*Amtiyaka*) as his immediate neighbour (*Anta*). Asoka's rule of these foreign territories is further proved by the unimpeachable evidence of an inscription located by him at a place called Sheri-Kula in the province of Arachosia (Kandahar). The only addition he made to this empire was Kalinga which he conquered by a bloody war against an unconquered (*avijita*) people cultured and socially advanced, whose heroic defence of their liberties against the aggressor resulted in colossal carnage and casualties in dead, wounded and captives. This bloody battle wrought at once a moral revolution in Asoka who forthwith forswore all war as an absolute evil and changed completely from the cult of violence to that of *Ahimsa* or Non-violence.

Thus Asoka's title to greatness was not only territorial but moral, not merely the geographical extent of his empire, but rather the principles of its administration. He stands out as the pioneer of Peace, peace between man and man, and between man and every sentient creature, for the sanctity of life and for abolition of violence in every sphere, domestic and foreign, internal and international. He organised measures for the relief of suffering of men and animals by provision of medical treatment (*chikitsa*) with medicine derived from sources such as "herbs, roots and fruits" (*aushadha-mula-phala*) obtained by import where necessary and also by cultivation in the country of medicinal plants in specialised botanical gardens or plantations (RE II). In his Rock Edict, III, he reports that his humanitarian measures were making good progress in the country and also in the States on its frontiers (the *Antas*), while his religion of universal brotherhood impelled him to despatch to the more prominent foreign, western countries fully equipped medical missions charged with the duty of introducing to them these measures of social service and welfare. The kings of these Western European countries who were his contemporaries are mentioned by him in the Inscriptions (RE II and XIII) as follows:

(i) Antiochus Theos II *(Amtiyoko nama Yana Raja)* (261-246 B.C.) of Syria;

(ii) Ptolemy II Philadelphos *(Turamaye)* (285-247 B.C.) of Egypt;

(iii) Antigonos Gonatas *(Amtikini)* (278-239 B.C.) of Macedon;

(iv) Magas *(Maka)* (300-250 B.C.) of Cyrene; and

(v) Alexander *(Alikasudaro)* (273-258 B.C.) of Epirus.

As to the States on his frontiers within the purview of

his humanitarian work, RE II mentions the Cholas, Pandyas, Keralaputras (modern Kerala State) and Satiaputras of the South up to Tamraparni (Ceylon); in the north west, Yonas, Kambojas, and others; and in the interior Bhojas, Pitinikas, Andhras and Palidas.

From the measures for the relief of bodily suffering by treatment of physical diseases, Asoka went on to apply his idealism to a wider sphere, that of relieving mankind itself from the scourge and suffering of war. He now proposed the outlawry and abolition of war itself as an absolute evil (*adharma*) and replacing bloody conquests by what he calls *Dharma-Vijaya*, the conquest of righteousness, the Triumph of Truth which is won by the willing consent of the conquered to be converted to this new doctrine in a feeling of spontaneous devotion (*priti-rasa*). He declared that "there should not be any fresh conquest of violence" (*navam vijayam ma vijetavya*). He applied this doctrine of Peace first to himself by stopping with the conquest of Kalinga as his last conquest in life. Asoka was thus the first in history to declare for abolition of war as the foundation of universal Peace, and to apply to his own empire the principles that he preached. These principles humanity has been still struggling to attain through international institutions like the League of Nations, and its successor, the UNO. Asoka was thus far ahead of his age in his moral and political idealism.

He was now more anxious to preach peace and spread morals than to extend his territory. By his Peace and Welfare Missions, he was building up a larger spiritual dominion, a Kingdom of Righteousness, an empire of thought resting on the force of law, and not the law of force.

He now devoted himself most assiduously to the moral uplift of his people by creating a separate Ministry of Morals which embarked on a whirlwind campaign for mass instruction in righteousness. In his Inscriptions, he insists on the purity of the home and cultivation of domestic virtues as the foundation of religious life. He lays a new emphasis on the view that religion was more a matter of conduct and character (*dharma-mangala*) than rituals and ceremonies (RE IX). He points out (RE XI) that the best of gifts (*dharma-dana*) was not that of material perishable goods but the gift of character (RE XI). In a country of multiplicity of sects and creeds, he emphasised toleration as the primary religion which must recognise that there is a *sara* or essence which is common to all religions, a universal moral standard as their fundamental basis. This spirit of toleration is to be cultivated by followers of different religions by (1) coming together in assemblies (*samavaya*) to discuss their different doctrines in a breadth of outlook (*bahuka*); (2) studying their different religious texts as a *Bahusruta* and (3) restraining thoughtless criticism (*vachoguti*) (RE XII).

But Asoka was not merely an idealist and a religious reformer. He was also great as a builder. He was builder of cities and palaces, of *stupas* and *viharas*, of rock-cut caves, and monolithic pillars and also of public works of utility of different kinds.

The Chinese traveller, Fa-hien, seeing his Palace at Pataliputra after a lapse of over 600 years, saw "the royal palace and halls still existing now as of old, and as the work not of men but of spirits which piled up the stones, reared the walls and gates, and executed the elegant curving and inlaid sculpture work in a way which no human hand of this world could accomplish" (my *Asoka*, p. 95)

He built *stupas* as high as peaks of hills (*girisringa kalpaih*) as described by the *Divyavadana*.

He had caves cut as the abode of ascetics in the Khalatika hills of Barabar and Nagarjuni near Gaya, with their walls shining like mirrors.

The polish of the Asokan pillar is "the despair of modern masons" (Marshall). It was so shining that Tom Coryat and Whittaker (Kerr's *Voyages and Travels*, IX, p. 423) coolly described it as "a pillar of brass", Chaplain Terry as "a pillar of marble", and Bishop Heber as one of "cast metal".

The pillar also is an example of the art of dressing, chiselling, and shaping of stones. The capitals of the columns were shaped into figures of animals which Marshall considers as "masterpieces in point of both style and technique, examples of finest carving".

The location of the pillars at their appointed sites presented a difficult problem of transport. They were huge monolithic shafts with a weight of 50 tons and height of 50 ft., which were hewn out of the neighbouring quarries of Chunar hills, fashioned at the central workshop at Pataliputra and transported to distances of 1,000 miles to be located at distant places like Meerut. The *Tarikhi-Firozshahi* states that Sultan Firoz Shah Tughlak, to remove the Asokan Pillar from Topra (Ambala) to Delhi, had to employ the labour force of 8,400 men pulling at the 42 wheels of a car to carry it. But, according to the Persian MS, *Sirat-i-Firozshahi* of A.D. 1370 (20th year of Firoz Shah's reign), elephants were first tried, and then 20,000 men for carrying the pillar to the river, placing it on boats and for subsequent operations ending in its re-erection at Firozabad in Delhi (See *Arch. Memoir* No. 52 on Kotla Firoz Shah). Firoz Shah also removed to Delhi the other pillar from Meerut.

Mauryan engineering was thus quite up to solving these difficult problems of transport and haulage of stupendous weights by suitable mechanical contrivances.

It has also to its credit the construction of the earliest reservoir and dam for irrigation in India in Saurashtra. According to the Inscription of the Saka King Rudradaman I of 150 A.D. a beautiful lake (*Tataka*) aptly called *Sudarsana* was constructed on the hills named Raivataka and Urjayat in the Saurashtra Province of the Maurya Empire with its governor (Rashtriya) named Pushyagupta Vaisya under emperor Chandragupta Maurya. The reservoir was created by damming up the flow of the hill streams Suvarnasikata, Palasini and others and equipped with "conduits (*pranali*), drains, and means to guard against foul matters" by the Yavana Governor of Saurashtra named Tushaspha under Asoka.

Lastly, Asoka's greatness is proved by his solicitude for the welfare of the masses and the travelling public by the construction of public works of utility which included "(a) planting of shade-giving banyan trees and groves of mango trees on the high-ways, (b) providing wells (*Udupana*) at every half *kos* of the roads (c) construction of rest houses (*nishadya*) and (d) providing watering places (*apana*) for use of men and cattle" (PE VII and RE II).

Asoka is also unique in leaving behind him a record of his work in Inscriptions which read like his autobiography. The Inscriptions are incised on stone, on rock and pillar to be read as his permanent proclamations of righteousness by the masses for whose convenience they were located and distributed all over his far-flung empire from Kandahar, Shahbhaz Garhi, and Mansehra in the North-west to Mysore in the South, Kalsi in the North, Dhauli in Eastern India, and Maski and Kurnool in the Deccan.

CHAPTER IX

ART

ART was rather late in coming. It was because the thought, the religion that creates Art was not quite favourable to it. Vedic thought, as we have seen, laid stress on the concept of the Atman as the Sole and Ultimate Reality, the Absolute, the Infinite, the Formless, while Art arises from the contrary mental process of seeking to render the Infinite in terms of Form and Finite, the Visible and Tangible. Art is interested in the manifestations of the One in the many, the Concrete and the Objective as represented in an endless variety of individual forms and expressions. In a word, one may generalise and say that while Religion aims at the expansion of the Individual progressively into the Universal, Art seeks to express the Universal and the Absolute in terms of the Individual and the Concrete, with its appeal to the bodily senses.

Indian art, however, had its start in the non-Aryan world, in the Indus Civilization, of which a glimpse has been given in an early chapter. We may just recall here a few of its artistic creations: (1) The two mutilated torsos of Harappa, the naked torso in red sandstone of a man, showing the modelling of mature sculpture, and the other, the figure in grey slate of a dancing male in action, a body in movement, with its unique fleshy emphasis.

(2) The two Statuettes, one figuring the *Yogi* in contemplation, with his eyes fixed on the tip of the nose, in steatite, and the other, the figure in bronze of a dancing girl, showing in its modelling a rare sensuous quality. (3) The figures

of animals on Seals, the best being the humped bull, showing most vividly the majesty and restrained vigour of the animal in the best style of naturalistic art.

Although Vedic Religion did not encourage art, its ceremonial needs gave some scope to it. Vedic sacrifice was performed on altar (*yajnavedi*) in a Hall (*yajnasala*). The *Vedi* was built in different forms, like "a falcon," "chariot," or "man with uplifted arms" as stated in the *Taittiriya Samhita*, thus giving scope to design. A Vedic fire-altar has been traced at Cannanore and Vedic rock-cut tombs near Tellicherry. Supposed Vedic burial mounds have been unearthed at Nandangarh in Bihar, together with the content of a small gold leaf upon which was impressed the figure of a nude female taken to be the Earth Goddess of the Vedic burial hymns. There have been found several terracotta images of this Goddess wearing a girdle. According to the *Atharvaveda* (VI 133, 5), the girdle was an amulet charged with a charm for longevity (*dirghayutva*) and was worn by the Rishis (*rishayah paribedhire*) as its symbol. Thus the inference may be made that images of this Goddess wearing the *Mekhala* were made in the time of the *Atharvaveda*. The *Vajasaneyi Samhita* (XI-XVIII) refers to an altar made of 10,800 bricks and shaped like a bird with outspread wings, with some amount of architectural skill. The *Rigveda* (IV, 24, 10) refers to an image of god Indra fetching the price of 10 coins.

The Vedic metaphysical trend towards the abstract and the subjective influenced Indian thought for a long time. Even early Buddhism came under its spell. The Buddha banned his own portraiture lest the attention of his disciples is drawn more to his physical body than to the truths he preached. With him truth counted more than its seeker. But he could not suppress the urge of the natural. He could not ban his indirect worship by symbols which were of three classes: (1) *Saririka*, symbols which 'pertained to his body', e.g., his head dress which is enshrined in a domed temple in a Bharhut sculpture which is also labelled; (2) *Uddesika* or Monuments like (a) *Stupa* (b) Wheel (called *Dhamma-Chakra*) and (c) *Tri-ratna,* the Buddhist Trinity of the Buddha, Sangha, and Dharma; (3) *Pari-bhogika,* 'what was used by him', such as (a) the throne (*Bodhimanda*) used by him under the Bodhi Tree, (b) his footprints and (c) the Bodhi Tree.

There was also the widespread worship of the relics of his sacred cremated body. These were enshrined for regular worship in the monuments known as *Stupas,* as stated above.

Thus the *Stupa* emerged as the earliest form of Indian architecture. Its oldest example was that found at Piprahwa on Nepal border. It contained an urn which bore an inscription stating that "this Shrine for the relics of the Buddha, the August one, is the pious foundation (*sukiti*) of the Sakyas, His brethren, in association with their sisters, their children, and their wives."

Vincent Smith expressed the view that "the masonry of the *Stupa* is excellent of its kind, well and truly laid." As it was constructed by the Sakyas, it might have been one of the original eight *Stupas* in which were enshrined the sacred relics of the Buddha by their eight claimants who included the Sakyas.

Some examples of old Indian architecture have been traced to the time of King Bimbisara (c 603-515 B.C.) and King Ajatasatru (c 551-519 B.C.) of Magadha, contemporaries of the Buddha (c 623-543 B.C.). Old Rajagriha was the original capital of Bimbisara, with its cyclopaean walls and fortifications. He built another capital at New Rajagriha under his Architect named Mahagovinda. The first Buddhist Council (*Samgiti*) met, as we have seen, in the Sattapanni Cave which was equipped with a Hall "built with all speed at its entrance" by Ajatasatru.

We may next mention as examples of pre-Maurya Art the group of colossal statues numbering about 13 so far discovered. They are figures of the minor deities of popular folk-religion of those days, Deities known as Yakshas, Yakshis, Nagas, Nagis, Gandharvas, Apsaras, Tree and Water-spirits, and the like. Five of these statues bear Inscriptions which name (1) Yaksha Manibhadra, (2) Yakshi Layava, (3) Bhagavan Akshata-nivika (Kubera) and (4) Yaksha Sarvatra-Nandi, while one Statue presents the names of the Master-craftsman Gomitaka, his son Kunika, and his son Naka, constituting a School of Sculptors of three generations. These were *Gramas-Silpis* as Panini calls them, as distinguished from the Court Artists called *Raja-Silpis*. These produced the art of Asoka, while the rural craftsmen were contributing to folk-art inspired by folk-religion. According to Coomaraswamy, these Statues are "informed by an astounding physical energy not obscured by their archaic stiffness, and expressive of an immense material force in terms of sheer volume, an art of mortal essence, without any suggestion of subjectivity or spiritual aspiration." This type is later continued in the colossal statues of the Bodhisattva like that on view at Sarnath Museum, and bearing an inscription describing it as the gift of Friar Bala in year 81 A.D. (=3 of Emperor Kanishka I). There is also an image of Mathura Bodhisattva at the Lucknow Museum. On the same lines was fashioned the colossal standing statue of Emperor Kanishka I on view at the Mathura Museum.

Asoka was a great builder, the builder of cities, palaces, cave-dwellings, *stupas*, and pillars. The material of his architecture was stone quarried in the Chunar hills. His palace at Pataliputra was seen more than six centuries later by the Chinese Pilgrim, Fa-hien, in its pristine magnificence described by him as "the work of spirits who piled up the stones, reared the walls and gates, and executed the elegant carving and inlaid sculpture-work in a manner which no mortal hands could accomplish". He was also the first to excavate dwellings in the hard granitic rocks of Barabar and Nagarjuni hills near Gaya. His Pillars show a high standard of workmanship as monoliths of sandstone showing a polish which "no modern mason can produce" (Marshall). Their capital gave scope to art in its several parts, viz., (1) the bell or lotus surmounted by (2) an *abacus* carved with figures of animals and foliage, (3) four lions set back to back as in Sarnath Pillar and (4) the big wheel of Dharma, with 32 spokes, placed on their shoulders. These details of decoration are based on design suggested by religion. The lotus is the symbol of the unfolding of the soul. The animals are associated with the turning points of the Buddha's life, as already explained. The wheel on the beasts of burden shows the supremacy of the spiritual over the physical. The 32 spokes stand for the 32 marks of the Superman (*Mahapurushalakshanam*) as stated in Buddhist texts.

Marked progress in art is next seen in the *Stupas* of Bharhut and Sanchi, and the carving on their railings and gateways. The Bharhut sculptures depict scenes of the Buddha's previous lives as narrated in the *Jatakas*, and also events in his life on earth. They also represent the folk-religion of the times in figures of Yakshas and Yakshis, Nagas and Nagis, and other godlings already mentioned. They also depict scenes of secular life, education in the hermitages, economic life of the common man, royal processions headed by elephants and horses, ponds teeming with lotuses, water-fowl and fish, fruit, flowers, and foliage, expressive of a general feeling for Nature and animal life and interest in robust mundane existence not dominated by the spiritual. They show medallions of beautiful female faces and even a woman as standard-bearer on horse-back, serving in cavalry. There is also a scene of dental surgery operated with a pair of forceps by monkey and elephant. The labelled royal scenes associated with kings Ajatasatru and Prasenajit, are unique contributions made by art to history. Two of its sculptures are noteworthy as narrative reliefs. The first is the *Mriga-Jataka* medallion showing how a royal hunter is cured of his violence by a stag.

The second depicts the descent of the Celestial Elephant into the womb of Buddha's mother, Mayadevi, in her dream, as she sleeps on a cot with a lamp burning at night.

The Bharhut Sculptures also continue the art of the statuary by executing large portraits of Yakshas, Yakshis, Nagas, and Devatas which are labelled as follows: (1) Kubera on man (*Naravahana*), (2) Gangito Yakho on an elephant, (3) Suchiloma Yakho, (4) Erapato Nagaraja bowing to the Buddha (5) Chada (Chamda) Yakhi on a *makara*, (6) Chakavako Nagaraja adoring the Buddha, (7) Yakhini Sudasana on a *makara*, (8) Chulakoka Devata on an elephant, (9) Mahakoka Devata, Goddess of hunting, (10) Sirima Devata and (11) *Sri*, upon whom two elephants pour water.

Bharhut was followed by the Great *Stupa* of Sanchi, with its elaborately-carved gateways showing a marked sculptural advance. One of its scenes is unique as an expression of religious romance. It represents the fateful event of Gautama's Renunciation (*abhinishkramanam*) by flight from the palace on the riderless horse, with umbrella on saddle as a symbol of Gautama's spiritual sovereignty, and with their hoofs held in the palm of their hands by the gods who muffled their sound lest it roused the city from slumber to frustrate the flight. The gods conspired with the horse for the success of the Renunciation upon which depended the future of mankind! The Gateways of Sanchi erected under patronage of Andhra kings are adorned with relics depicting events in the Buddha's life, a few *Jataka* stories, figuring Yakshas and Yakshis, animals, decorative designs, and Buddhist symbols. While Bharhut shows 30 *Jataka* stories, Sanchi shows only 6. There are also scenes of common life in that age. A supposed historical scene is Asoka's visit to the withering Bodhi tree on which he poured water for its revival, as stated in the *Divyavadana*. Another scene depicts a boat being rowed by three devotees to the rescue of the Buddha at sea.

A few Bodh Gaya reliefs form a chronological link between Bharhut and Mathura. So also are the rock-cut reliefs of some early Chaitya caves like Bhaja. The caves are hewn out of solid rock to provide Assembly Halls. This early rock cutting culminated later in the Caves and Temples of Ajanta and Elura.

We now come to Mathura as the next centre of Art during the first three centuries of the Christian era. It became at once a commercial, cultural, political and religious centre as one of the chief cities of the Kushana empire. It was at the junction of the main trade routes which linked up Pataliputra with Taxila and the north-west and also with the port of Bharukachchha on the west coast. It was also the meeting place of three cultural streams, Brahminical, Jain, and Buddhist and their artistic traditions.

Though Buddhist art was predominant in that early age, it did not mean the extinction of Brahminical art. A glimpse of it is found in the column erected in the time of the Sungas at Besnagar (Bhilsa) by a Greek Hindu in honour of Vasudeva, the God of Gods (*Deva-deva*), as his devotee (*Bhagavata*). But here also the God was not portrayed, as in Buddhism, but only his symbol, the *Garudadhvaja*. Again, the Grammarian Patanjali, writing in the 2nd century B.C., recalls the practice of the Mauryas in making for sale images of deities, Siva, Skanda and Visakha, as profitable business (*Mauryaih hiranyarthivih archah prakalpitah*).

The Kushana period saw the great Schism splitting up Buddhism into the two Schools or Sects known as *Hinayana* and *Mahayana*. The Kushana kings were patrons of Mahayana. The schism had its consequences to art. There was a great demand for Buddhist images for worship. *Mahayana* presented a new pantheon comprising (1) The Buddha now worshipped as a god, (2) the previous human Buddhas, (3) the Dhyani Buddhas of the four Quarters, (4) the Bodhi sattvas as their spiritual sons and (5) their feminine consorts called Taras.

The Mathura workshops were kept busy in meeting this widespread demand for images. Examples of Mathura work have been found at Taxila in the north-west, and also at Sarnath, Gaya and Pataliputra. But this demand was also met by a new School of Art called Gandhara School.

The Gandhara School catered for the religious requirements of a large area from its centre at Taxila. Besides Taxila and Peshawar areas, Gandhara sculptures are found in areas in Afghanistan such as Bamiyan, Jalalabad and Hadda. Bamiyan is a place of pilgrimage with its innumerable monasteries, and caves, colossal Buddha statues carved *in situ* in the rock, one of which reaches up to a height of 175 feet.

The Gandhara School fashioned the Buddha image after the Greek pattern with its spirit of realism. Western art tends to representation, while Indian to symbolism. Thus it produced the emaciated Buddhas or the Buddhas with moustache.

The Buddha image first appeared in Gandhara in the first century A.D. The Buddha image of the Indian type also emerged about the same time in Mathura.

It is the type of a *Yogi* seated, cross-legged, in meditation, in *padmasana*, under the Bodhi Tree. This ascetic type is first seen in its perfect form in a Bharhut sculpture which bears the label: "The Yogi who practised austerities for years (*Dirgha tapasvi*) now instructs his pupils (*sisc anusasati*)." This was the prototype of the later Buddha images which correspond to its pattern. Thus the Buddha image was the creation of indigenous Indian art.

At Mathura met different cultural streams and artistic traditions. Here are found Buddhist *Stupas*, complete with railings and gateways, Jain and Brahmanical shrines, figures of Jain Tirthankaras and Hindu Gods and Goddesses. A Jain *Stupa* has been excavated at Mathura with railing pillars decorated with nude Yakshis associated with trees.

A "tablet of homage" has also been found, with a relief of a Jain Stupa. The popular Hindu folk-religion is represented by the figures of Kubera and his Bachchanalian group and of Yakshas and Nagas. There are representations of Naga cult among the Mathura sculptures which are thus very comprehensive in their scope and hospitable to all cults.

While the Kushana kings were patronising the art of Mathura, the first of the classical monuments of the South was being built and carved under the Andhra kings of the Deccan. It was the *Stupa* of Amaravati in Guntur district of Andhrapradesa of about 200 B.C. but its rails were later, of about 150-250 A.D. Most of the *Stupa* and its railings had been reduced to rubble till 160 of the finest sculptures were salvaged and brought to England where they are in the custody of the British Museum. The Amaravati carvings continue the bas-relief tradition of Bharhut and Bodh Gaya. They present images of the Buddha in human form, together with the old symbols. There are found two marble statues of the Buddha showing the treatment of the drapery hanging in loose folds after Gandharan technique. At the same time, the figure of the Buddha is intensely "ascetic and severe, representing pure thought rather than design." Each image was still an individual achievement and iconography is not yet rigidly evolved. Specially noteworthy is the fine rendering of flower and foliage, and the medallions and panelled friezes illustrating the Buddha legend in the narrative method of Gandhara art as reflected in Mathura work.

After Andhra and Kushana, we come to the Age of the Guptas. The Gupta Empire was a well-organised State which achieved the political unification of the country and strengthened its cultural unity based on the comprehensive system known as Hinduism as expounded in the great Epic of *Mahabharata*, giving scope to different schools of thought. "A fundamental unity of experience and character transcends all political, racial, linguistic, and sectarian distinctions." A new philosophy came to view the forms and experiences of finite life as revelations of the Infinite. Popular worship was now rationalised and given formal sanction by the philosophical mind. Buddhism is now completely fused with the national life, with the Buddha himself being assimilated into the Brahmanic pantheon as an incarnation of Vishnu. The Buddha figure now forms an integral part of architecture.

Art was now even the hobby of royalty and not a mere vocational and hieratic production. The Gupta emperor, Samudra Gupta, was a 'prince of poets' (*Kaviraja*), and also played on the *Vina*, as portrayed on his coins.

Art was now completely Indianised and emancipated from all foreign influence. That influence flowed from the West, but now India is herself spreading her influence abroad, towards the Far East by way of Central Asia, and Further India and Indonesia by sea.

At home, Art now centred round the representative Deities of different religions, Vishnu (or Krishna), Siva, Sakti, Buddha or Bodhisattva, patronised impartially by the Gupta kings who were personally Vaishnavas and called themselves *parama bhagavatas*. Images and temples appropriate to each of these persuasions of Hinduism appear in profusion.

We may now refer to a few typical examples of these.

The Temple of Bhitargaon (of sixth century A.D.) in Kanpur district is profusely decorated with carved brickwork and terracotta panels depicting *Saiva* themes. The Deogarh Temples in Jhansi shows a figure of Siva as a *Yogi*, which is considered as a masterpiece. A cave-temple at Udayagiri dated to 401 A.D. shows fine sculptures of Vishnu as Varaha, of Goddess Ganga on Makara, and Yamuna on *Kachchhapa*. In the neighbouring temple at Pathari, there is a massive relief on the nativity of Krishna, which is supposed by Beglar as "the finest and largest piece of Indian Sculpture." The Deogarh temple also has a panel showing Vishnu resting on Ananta.

The temple of Bhumara shows an image of Surya dressed like the Kanishka Statue of Mathura Museum without his horses.

Inscription No. 17 of Fleet's *Gupta Inscriptions* refer to a temple for the worship of the seven Divine Mother along with an image of Sakti in the form of Mahishamardini. The Bihar Stone Pillar Inscription of Skanda Gupta mentions a group of temples (*Devaniketana mandalam*) dedicated to the Divine Mothers including Bhadrarya, name of Parvati.

The dancing Siva type decorates the Durga temple at Aihole of 5th century A.D.

The Badami caves close by include a Saiva temple in Cave I, Vaishnava temples in Caves II and III, and a Jain temple in Cave No. IV.

The outstanding monuments of the period may be classified into three main groups: (1) Ajanta and Ellora in the Deccan, (2) Badami including the temples at Aihole and Pattadkal and (3) Mamallapuram on Madras Coast.

The Caves at Ajanta are Buddhist. They include both *Viharas* or Monasteries and *Chaityas* or Assembly-halls. The *Vihara* includes a shrine for private worship.

The earliest caves at Ellora are dated to about A.D. 500. The masterpiece of Ellora is the eighth century Kailasa Temple dedicated to Siva. The entire temple is cut out of the rock. The surrounding walls and the sides of the temple are profusely carved with images of popular Deities, animals, and scenes from the Epics. The sculptures of Ellora are conspicuous for their remarkable life-quality. "Although drawn directly from nature, this art is never, in the narrow imitative sense, naturalistic. The texture is not that of flesh but of stone; and the animation that seems to spring from the sculptured figures comes not from any mere linear dexterity but from energies revealed in the rock itself and the play of light upon it. The Kailasa sculptors tried to create the effect of movement and cut their figures in deep relief to achieve this end."

The best relief shows Siva and Parvati on Mount Kailasa being shaken by Ravana from within, and steadied by Siva with mere pressure of his foot. Coomaraswamy thinks that the sculpture represents "the forces of strain and resistance at work in the earth's crust." Another represents the River Goddesses, Ganga, Yamuna, and Sarasvati.

The Pallava monuments at Mamallapuram include seven monolithic shrines cut from granite boulders on the seashore and a superb open-air bas-relief carved on a slab of rock with figures of gods, men, and animals of all kinds. There is a scene of Arjuna's penance but it might be that of Bhagiratha moving by his prayer the Ganga down from heaven to earth, released from the locks of Siva.

The Gupta period is also known for its finished form of temple architecture marked by (1) pyramidal tower (*Sikhara*) built over (2) the cellar sanctum, or shrine, (3) porticos supported on pillars and (4) door-way decorated with carvings. Among the best examples of temples may be mentioned (1) the Vishnu Temple at Tigawa (Jabalpur), (2) the Siva Temple at Bhumara noted for its sculptures, medallions showing *Kirtimukhas*, figures of Ganesa, Brahma, Yama, Kubera, Kartikeya, Siva dancing on Bull, Surya, Kama and Mahishasuramardini, practically illustrating the entire Hindu pantheon and (3) the Parvati Temple at Nachna.

Gupta art also revived the free standing Pillars. The Buddha Gupta Pillar of A.D. 484 at Eran is surmounted by a lion-abacus and a statuette of Vishnu at the top. The Iron Pillar at Delhi, 23′ 8″ high, composed of pure malleable iron is cast in one piece and weighs more than 6 tons, "a technical feat unparalleled in Europe until many centuries later."

Among the best Gupta sculptures may be noted (1) the Mathura standing Buddha with a decorated *sirashchakra*,

(2) Mankuwar Seated Buddha dated to A.D. 446 and (3) seated Buddha of Sarnath. . To these may be added the sculptures of Deogarh Temple showing (1) Four-armed Vishnu Seshasayi, (2) Brahma, (3) Indra, (4) Kartikeya, (5) Siva and Parvati on Nandi, (6) Five Pandavas with Draupadi, (7) Nara-Narayana and (8) Gajendramoksha. Mention may also be made of the colossal copper statue of the Buddha found at Sultanganj (now in the Birmingham Museum).

After the Gupta period, there were constructed many noteworthy temples of which the following were most prominent, viz., (1) the Lingaraja Temple of Bhuvanesvara considered to be the finest example of a Hindu temple, with its lofty tower imposing beyond words, and sculptural details of great beauty; (2) the Black pagoda of Konarak, temple of the Sun (*Arka*) in the form of a car borne on immense wheels drawn by horses, Surya's *Vahanas*, abounding in erotic sculptures "representing an aspect of life to exclude which will be a denial of God"; (3) the Kandarya Mahadeva Temple at Khajuraho equally full of erotic sculptures; (4) the Dilwara Jain Temple on Mt. Abu, with its delicate and intricate sculpture in white marble (anticipating the art of the Taj); and (5) the Hoyasalesvara Temple at Halebid, with its companion Temple at Belur, most richly ornamented with sculptures illustrating the entire Indian Mythology.

We may in conclusion note the evolution of the Hindu Temple out of the Buddhist *Stupa* in stages. The *Stupa*, as we have seen, originated in the religious demand for enshrining for purposes of worship the relics of the Buddha. Next we see how in the caves of Karle and Nasik, which were constructed as the Viharas or residential quarters for monks, the *Stupa* came to be located in the apse at the end of their quandrangular hall which was divided by Pillars into a naive and aisles. In the third stage, the apse is changed into a closed cellar or shrine where were installed the image of a Deity in place of the Buddhist relic. The cellar was fitted with a door, while the pillared space in front of the apse now became a roofed porch called a *Mandapa*. The position of a cellar in the temple is marked out from the outside by a spire known as *Sikhara* and the two together formed what was known as its *Vimana*. The whole now becomes the Hindu Temple which thus arose out of the *Stupa* as its origin.

Paintings.—The oldest paintings are probably those of Jogimara Caves on Ramgarh Hills in Surguja State (M.P.) and may be dated to about second century B.C. The most famous paintings are to be found in the caves of Ajanta numbering 29, with four *Chaityas* and the rest as *Viharas*. The paintings cover the period from first to seventh century A.D. and attained a high standard of art so as to influence the art of Asia and, indeed, of all countries into which Buddhism had penetrated. "They bear comparison with the best that Europe could produce down to the time of Michael Angelo." They were executed on the walls of rock-hewn shrines in sites far out of the way. This explains their preservation. Their subjects are scenes from the life of the Buddha, and the *Jatakas*, e.g. defeat of Mara, Bodhisattva, Indra and Sachi, Buddha Triad, Great renunciation, Seven Buddhas and story of Sibi. A feeling for animals and birds expresses itself in the deer and birds of Ajanta paintings. Specially artistic is the Ajanta painting of the majestic over-sized figure of the Bodhisattva, with its profound pathos and divine dignity which cannot be missed.

At Bagh, in Gwalior district, are found some cave paintings of about sixth or seventh century A.D. resembling Ajanta style. Its naturalistic trend is seen in the great elephant procession. The Ajanta style is also to be seen in Sigiriya in Ceylon in its series of 21 beautiful female figures painted on the walls of its rock chambers.

The influence of Indian painting is also seen in the discoveries made in Central Asia by explorers like Sir Aurel Stein, of numerous wall-paintings and pictures upon wooden panels, silk, and other fabrics.

CHAPTER X

COINAGE

THE evolution of coinage in ancient India is marked by three stages. At first, there was the metallic currency of various forms, without any stamp to indicate its official issuing authority. Then came what are called punch-marked coins made of pieces of metal of different shapes and weights, which were punch-marked with tokens and letters notifying their value, and the authority issuing and guaranteeing them. Generally, these coins were square or oblong pieces cut out of silver, with the marks of the money-changers punched on to them on the obverse, while the marks on the reverse indicated the locality of their origin. The oldest coins are dated to about fourth Century B.C.

But literary, especially Buddhist, texts mention earlier uses of coins for which the term was *Kahapana=Karshapana*. There were also known coins of gold called *Nikkha* and *Suvanna*, along with bronze or copper tokens called *kamsa*, *pada*, *masaka* (*masha*) and *kakanika*. The Vedic work, *Brihadaranyaka Upanishad*, tells how king Janaka paid his royal prize to Rishi Yajnavalkya in 5 *padas* of gold attached to each of the horns of 1,000 cows given away to him. Again, the *Vinaya* (III. 45) states: "At that time (of Bimbisara and Ajatasattu), at Rajagaha, five *masakas* were equal to one *pada*." The term *Nishka* is also a Vedic term for a gold coin.

In the third stage, there was a regular coinage of gold, silver, lead, billon and various alloys, while the old punch-marks were integrated into regular types, cast or struck from dies, and bearing Inscriptions and portraits of the authorities associated with them. In the meanwhile, in the fifth century B.C., Persian coins came into the north-west of India then under Achaemenid control, and these influenced Indian currency. The Persian gold *daric* first came and was supplanted by the cheaper silver coins called *Sigloi* (shekels) which influenced the indigenous silver coins, the punch-marked square pieces. Then came the period of Macedonian influence which brought to India Athenian *Owl* coins. Silver drachms of Attic weight (58 grains) were also imitated by the Indian king Saubhuti (Sophytes). An interesting silver decadrachm shows on the reverse a supposed portrait of Alexander, and on obverse an elephant bearing two riders, one of whom drives a lance into a pursuing horseman. It is taken by Head to depict defeated Porus on his state elephant aiming his javelin at the traitor King Ambhi galloping after him on horse.

We may now describe some actual specimens of select ancient Indian coins. Old cast coins are found at the village of Eran in Saugor District. One of these bears on obverse the legend *Rano Dharna-palasa*, '(coin) of King Dharmapala' written in old Brahmi script from right to left like Kharoshthi. There is again found a Guild token bearing on obverse the legend Dujaka or *Dojcka* in Kharoshthi characters, while the reverse has the legend *Negama*=Merchants in Brahmi characters. An interesting round copper-piece of the Panchala country, perhaps of the Sunga Dynasty, bears on obverse a figure on a lotus, and on reverse the Brahmi inscription *phagunimitrasa*=of Phalgunimitra. Mention may also be made of an ancient coin struck from a single die showing on obverse (1) a *chaitya* or Buddhist shrine; (2) to left, the legend *Vatasvaka* in Brahmi; (3) to right, a standing figure in worship; and (4) beneath him, the symbol called *Nandi-pada*, 'the foot-print of Nandi' (Siva's Bull). The legend *Vatasvaka* may denote the *Vata* (fig-tree) branch of the Asvakas of the north-west who fought Alexander and were called by the Greeks *Assakenoi*.

We now come to the period of the Greek kings who ruled over portions of Afghanistan and the Punjab from *c*. 250 B.C. to *c*. 25 B.C. Their coins bring to light 35 Kings and 2 Queens most of whom are unknown otherwise. The coins bear on obverse the name and title of the king in Greek script and on reverse their equivalents in Indian script and dialect, thereby supplying a valuable key and clue to the Indian script and alphabet of those days.

We may now describe some of the select coins of this class which is a valuable source of Indo-Greek history.

1. Coin of Indian king *Sophytes* (=Sans. Saubhuti) who ruled over a kingdom in the Punjab at the time of Alexander's invasion. The coin shows on obverse the helmeted head of the king to right in the Greek style, and on reverse cock to right; above, on left, a caduceus; and Greek legend, *Sophutou*='(coin) of Sophytes.' In the Greek account, Sophytes entertained Alexander by the demonstration of a fight between a lion and four of his dogs set against it. From his sporting habits, we may suppose the cock on the coin as a fighting cock.

2. *Antialkidas* (c 110-80 B.C.) whose coin (of silver) shows on obverse (1) Bust of King to right, (2) Greek legend, *Basileos nikephorou Antialkidou*, 'coin of king Antialkidas, the Victorious'; and on reverse (a) Zeus seated on a throne and holding in his right hand a figure of Nike (the Goddess of Victory *Jayadhara;* (b) on the left, the forepart of an elephant, with trunk upraised; and (c) Kharoshthi legend, *'Maharajasa Jayadharasa Antialikitusa*? Antialkidas is the only Greek king who is mentioned in an Indian inscription. Other Greek kings are known only from their coinage. Antialkidas is mentioned in an inscription on a pillar erected at Vidisa (Besnagar) by his ambassador named Heliodorus in honour of 'the god of gods' (*Devadeva*) Vasudeva, of

whom he was a devotee (*Bhagavata*). The Pillar is called *Garuda-dhvaja* with the figure of Garuda as the vehicle of Vishnu adorning its top. It is also stated that this Greek ambassador (*Yona-duta*) was deputed by his king to the Indian king called 'Kasiputra Bhagabhadra, the protector' (Trata) (=Sunga King Bhadra of the *Puranas*).

3. *Menander* (c. 115-90 B.C.). His coin in silver shows on obverse (1) Bust of king thrusting a spear to left, (2) Greek legend *Basileas soteros* Menandrou, '(coin) of King Menander, the Protector'; and on reverse (1) Athene hurling a thunderbolt to right and (2) Kharoshthi legend '*Maharajasa tratarasa Menadrasa*'.

4. *Demetrius*. (c. 190-160 B.C.). There is a square copper piece which shows on the obverse (1) head of the king covered by the head-dress of an elephant's scalp and a diadem and (2) a legend in Greek corresponding on the reverse to the Kharoshthi legend, *Maharajasa aparajitasa Demitriyasa*.

5. *Maues*. (c. 90 B.C.-20 A.D.). One of his coins on reverse has the Greek legend, *Basileos Mauou*, 'Coin of King Maues.' Maues struck his coins after those of Demetrius, showing that the Saka invaders dispossessed the Greek kings of their territories. The Saka satrap, Liaka Kusulaka of Taxila, imitated the coins of Eukratides, and the Satrap, Ranjubula, at Mathura, imitated the coins of the Greek kings, Strato I and II, ruling conjointly. These imitation coins retain their original Greek form with Greek legend on obverse and its Prakrit translation in Kharoshthi characters on reverse.

A copper piece of Maues (or Moga) has on its obverse the figure of Poseidon, and a Greek legend which on the reverse is translated in Kharoshthi into Prakrit *Rajatirajasa mahatasa* Moyasa. It also bears a female figure amid vines.

6. *Zeionises*. Another type of Saka mintage is the round silver coin issued by Zeionises. It bears on obverse the figure of a mounted satrap and a Greek legend which in

its Kharoshthi translation on reverse reads: "*Manigulasa Chhatrapasa putrasa Chhatrapasa Jihonisa.*"

It may be noted that similar coins were issued by the successors of Maues, Azis and Azilisis; of Vonones and Spalgadama, who ruled in Arachosia and Drangiana; of the northern satraps, Rajuvula and Sondasa of Mathura; and also some others. The families of Vonones and Maues, the Pahlavas and Sakas, were closely connected, as shown by their coins. On some coins, Spalirises, brother of Vonones, is associated with Azes, the successor of Maues. The Indo-Parthians, Gondophernes (A.D. 21) and his successors, also issued coins which are in a sense midway between the Saka coins and the Kushana mintages to follow.

7. *Dharaghosha,* King of Audumbara, issued a remarkable piece in silver of *c.* 100 B.C. unconnected with Greek or Saka coinage. It bears on obverse Kharoshthi legends: (1) around, *Mahadevasa rana Dharaghosha/Odumbarisa*= 'Coin of the Great Lord, King Dharaghosha, Prince of Audumbara; (2) across, *Visvamitra.* The obverse bears a standing figure, probably that of the Rigvedic Rishi, Visvamitra.

After these Indo-Greek, Indo-Scythian, and Indo-Parthian coins comes the *Imperial Kushana Coinage* which was a gold currency on the basis of one part of gold to twelve of silver in imitation of the normal rate prevailing in Syria and the Roman empire between *c.* 100 B.C. and A.D. 100, a period which helps to fix Kushana chronology on a numismatic basis. A typical specimen of Kushana coinage is a gold piece of Wema Kadphises II, son of Kozulo Kadphises, who founded the dynasty in the first century A.D. Its obverse bears Wema's bust, with a Greek legend, and reverse a figure of Siva, with trident, and deer-skin, and the Kharoshthi inscription *Maharajasa rajadirajasa sarvaloga-isvarasa Mahisvarasa Vima kathphisasa.*

The Kushana type is best seen in a gold piece of Kanishka I, bearing on obverse a full-length portrait of Kanishka in

Turki dress, and top-boots, beside a fire-altar, with an inscription in Greek letters, *Shaonanoshao Kaneshki Koshano*, 'the king of Kings, Kanishka the Kushan'. The reverse shows God Siva with four arms, holding hand-drum, pitcher, trident, and goat, with the legend *Oesho* in Greek letters. Kanishka's coinage is unique in its cosmopolitan outlook, reflecting the extent of his empire made up of so many nationalities whose Deities are portrayed on it. These may be thus indicated: (1) *Greek* Helios (Sun God), (2) *Iranian* Orlagno (Iranian Verathragna), (3) Mithro (Avestic Mithra), (4) Manaobaga (Persian Mana-Bago, Moon-God, (5) Boddo (*Buddha*); Saka-Mana-Bouda (Buddha Sakyamuni); Odyo Boychakama=Advaya Buddha Sakyamuni, (6) Oado=*Vedic* Vata; Horon=Vedic Varuna, (7) Brahminical or *Hindu* Deities: (a) Oesho (=Sans. Bhavesa=Siva), (b) Ride=Riddhi, (c) Sarapis=Yama, (d) Maasena=Mahasena, (e) Skanda Komaro, (f) Bizago=Visakha, (g) Skanda=Komaro-Bizago, (h) Ommo=Uma. It was thus left to the Kushanas to weld into one empire different nationalities such as the Greeks, Sakas, Pahlavas, and Hindus.

The next phase of numismatic history is represented by the two Dynasties of Saka Satraps. The first was founded in Western India by Bhumaka and Nahapana who called themselves as *Kshaharata* Kshatrapas, while the other was founded at Ujjayini by the *Kardamakas*, Chashtana, Rudradaman and his successors who ruled for about three centuries. They issued their coinage in silver and continued the Saka numismatic tradition in imitating the Greek models. Thus a silver piece of Nahapana depicts on obverse the head of the Satrap, with a Greek legend, and on reverse the semi-Sanskrit version in Brahmi letters *Rajno Kshahararatasa Nahapanasa* and in Kharoshthi, the Prakrit *Rano chhaharatasa Nahapanasa*.

These Kshaharata coins were initiated in the mintages of minor Dynasties like *Abhira* of Nasik and also to some extent by the *Andhras*. For instance, a leaden piece of the

Andhra King Vilivayakura Gautamiputra shows on obverse the symbol of a *Chaitya* or sanctuary for the relics of the Buddha, which also appears on the coins of Chashtana and his successors. On the reverse are figured bow and arrow with the Brahmi legend *Rano Gotamiputasa Vilivayakurasa.*

We now come to *Imperial Gupta Coinage* which was mainly in gold, and at first modelled on Kushana coinage, with its foreign features, which were gradually replaced by indigenous features till it was completely Indianised. It represents the peak of numismatic craftsmanship in its variety of designs and symbols giving great scope to art. The scheme is to portray the king on obverse and the relevant Goddess on reverse.

The features of Gupta Coinage are best illustrated by the coinage of Emperor Samudra Gupta.

The king wears as head-dress the Indian cap or turban instead of the Kushana peaked or conical head-dress. He also wears Indian ornaments and *dhoti*.

Kushana Ardochsho is replaced on reverse by Hindu goddesses: (1) Lakshmi associated with lotus, (2) Durga on Lion or holding pasa, (3) Ganga on Makara associated with the tiger, (4) Saraśvati associated with the *Vina.*

Another Indian feature is Garuda on standard as vehicle of Vishnu and associated with Lakshmi, signifying that the Gupta kings were Vaishnavas. The dwarf is an Indian symbol and attendant of the king. The *Asvamedha* is an Indian coin-type.

The Gupta coins depict the king in a variety of positions: shooting a tiger, lion, or rhino; playing on lyre; seated on high-backed couch; riding a horse or elephant; feeding a peacock; and holding a standard, bow and arrow, or battle axe. They also figure appropriate symbols: Altar, Tulasi plant, Chakra and Umbrella, besides Garuda and Dwarf aforesaid.

The *Asvamedha* type figures the Horse, and the Queen, with altar and *Yupa*.

The king and queen are together seen on Samudra Gupta's Chandra Gupta type as being married.

Skanda Gupta issued King-and-Lakshmi type.

The Pratapa type of Kumara Gupta I brings on obverse two females with the king between. His king-and-queen type shows king offering flowers to the queen.

The Gupta coins devised many original legends descriptive of the king's characteristics and achievements. Thus Samudra Gupta is (1) *apratiratha*, (2) *kritantaparasu*, (3) *ajita-rajajetajita*, (the unconquered conqueror of unconquered kings), (4) *sarvarajo chchhetta* or (5) *vyaghraparakrama*. Chandra Gupta II is (1) *simhavikrama*, (2) *chakravikrama* and (3) *parama bhagavata*. Kumara Gupta I is (1) *vyaghra-bala-parakrama*, (2) *simha-mahendra*, (3) *simhanihanta mahendra-gaja and* (4) *bharta khadgatrata*. Skanda Gupta is a *sudhanvi*.

A point of marked originality in the Gupta mintage is its design in depicting exciting scenes of royal big-game hunting. It is to be noted that these scenes are not of mere superficial sporting interest. They are possessed of a deep historical and political significance. The wild animals appearing on the coins are there as symbols of the regions which were annexed to the Gupta empire by its conquests. Thus Samudra Gupta's conquest of the Gangetic Valley is symbolised by the royal Bengal Tiger which dwelt in its forests. The Rhino-hunting scene of his coins points to parts of Assam which were conquered by him and are still the habitat of the Rhino. The conquest of Saurashtra by Chandra Gupta II is typified by the Lion as its denizen. Thus these coins signify these new conquests by their wild life.

Further, the Tiger of the coins is linked with the river Ganga associated with the swamps and forests as its abode, while the Lion of Chandra Gupta's coins is linked with Goddess Durga as Her *Vahana.*

A reference may be made now to the mintages of the South, where the punch-marked currency was longer in vogue than in the North. Pallava coins, modelled on Andhra, bear on reverse the Ship (as on Yajna Sri Coins), while others, in gold and silver, bear as type the maned Lion as the emblem of the Pallavas. The Pandyas first issued square coins and, later, round gold coins showing on obverse the Pandya symbol of a double fish. The Chera coins figure the emblem of the Bow. Chola coins before Rajaraja present on obverse the Tiger as the Chola emblem, together with the Pandya Fishes and the Chera Bow. Rajaraja issued a new type figuring on obverse the king standing, and on reverse the seated Goddess of the Kushana pattern. The Chalukyas issued coins of gold, figuring the Boar as their emblem. The Kadambas had their gold coins bearing the Lotus as their emblem. The mintages of other dynasties are not much known.

CHAPTER XI

THE UNIVERSITY OF NALANDA

THE *Mahavihara* (University) of Nalanda was one of the greatest achievements of ancient India in the field of education. The *Mahavihara* was so called because it was the central institution to which were affiliated the indivdual colleges called *Viharas* as units of residence.

Nalanda was built up as a post-graduate University for advanced study and research. Hither flocked foreign students from countries like Korea, Mongolia, Japan, China, Tukhara, Tibet and Ceylon, in search of higher learning of which it was then the most important centre in Asia.

It is fortunate that a fairly full account of Nalanda has been given by the two learned Chinese scholars named Yuan Chwang and I-tsing, on the basis of their personal knowledge of its working seen by them as its students in residence. The former liver at Nalanda for 5 years (635-640) A.D.), and the latter for as many as 10 years from 675 A.D.

In the time of Yuan chwang, the students of the University "always" numbered 8,500 who were taught by 1,510 teachers, so that each teacher was in charge of a group of 5 pupils to each of whom he could give his personal attention and instruction upon which depends the efficiency of education. The methods of mass-production cannot apply to education which aims at the making of man by a process of delicate individual treatment. The same reasonable ratio of the number of teachers to taught is being increasingly observed in modern educational institutions. For instance, the Massachusetts Institute of Technology employs 1,174 teachers to instruct its 4,874 students.

The method of learning in Nalanda was also quite modern. It was the method of discussion in seminars. It was most popular among pupils. As Yuan Chwang states, "learning and discussing they found the day too short; day and night they admonished each other, juniors and seniors, mutually helping to perfection." The Chinese pilgrim also states that the teachers delivered between them every day as many as 100 discourses on as many different subjects, "and the students attend those discourses without any fail even for a minute."

Admission to Nalanda as a centre of higher study was strict. It was in the hands of a Board of Specialists who carefully guarded the gates of learning as its *Dvara-panditas* (gate-keepers) by holding a strict entrance test. According to Yuan Chwang, "only two or three out of ten" could pass that test. "The majority, beaten by the difficulty of the problems set at the test, withdraw, even of those from abroad." This meant that only 20% could pass the entrance examination, and 80% failed.

The strictness of admission built up the reputation of Nalanda for its high standard as a seat of learning. As pointed out by the Chinese pilgrim, "foreign students come to Nalanda to put an end to their doubts." To count as a student of Nalanda was considered a great academic honour. As Yuan Chwang says, "those who stole the name of Nalanda brother were all treated with respect, wherever they went." I-tsing also states that at Nalanda "assemble eminent and accomplished men in crowds, discuss possible and impossible doctrines and, after having been assured of the excellence of their opinions by wise men, become far-famed for their wisdom." Thus Nalanda was a clearing house of truths.

Students specialised in their higher studies on the basis of their preparatory knowledge of the following five compulsory subjects, viz., (1) Grammar and Lexicography (*Sabdavidya*, Science of sounds and words, (2) Arts and Crafts (*Silpasthanavidya*), (3) Science of Medicine (*Chikitsavidya*) (4) Logic (*Hetuvidya*) and (5) Philosophy (*Adhyatmavidya*). The utility of medical science as a compulsory subject of study is thus explained by I-tsing: "Is it not a sad thing that sickness prevents the pursuit of one's duty and vocation? Is it not beneficial if people can benefit others as well as themselves by the study of medicine?"

Besides these compulsory subjects of study, Nalanda provided for instruction in all the learning then known, Brahminical or Buddhist, sacred and secular, philosophical and practical, sciences and arts. The Head of the University, Silabhadra by name, was the highest authority on the theory and practice of Yoga which Yuan Chwang came all the way from China, against the perils of that difficult journey by land-routes, to learn at the feet of its Master at Nalanda.

A singular feature of Nalanda education was that it Indianised the foreign students as far as possible. They dropped even their own (foreign) names and assumed in their place Indian names. Thus Hiuen Tchao become Prakasamati; Tao-hi, Srideva; a native of Tukharestan assumed the name of Buddhadharma; Tao-cheng became Chandradeva; Ta-cheng-teng became Mahayana-pradipa; Tao-lin, Silabhadra; and Ling-yun, Prajnadeva.

Foreign students had their own colleges for their residence and study at Nalanda. The most famous example of these was the college or *Vihara* founded for Javanese students (*Viharah Karitah*) by an endowment made by their king Balaputradeva, 'Lord of Suvarna-dvipa and Yava-bhumi', as recorded in an inscription of King Devapaladeva of Magadha of A.D. 854. The endowment provided for the students all their necessaries such as food (*pindapata*), clothing (*chivara*), accommodation (*satra*), beds (*sayanasana*), medicines (*bheshajyadi*), pens (*lekhanadi*) and religious needs (*bali* and *charu*). This college was known as a centre of Tantrika Buddhism.

Some of the masterminds and creative geniuses of India were teachers at Nalanda in different periods. Its president in Yuan Chwang's time was Silabhadra, a prince of Samatata (in South Bengal), who renounced the world to become a Yogi. The great Chemist Nagarjuna was a teacher at Nalanda for years, together with his famous pupil, Aryadeva, the founder of Madhyamika School of Buddhism. Here also "lived for 12 years" Asanga, the founder of the Yogachara School. He is said to have been followed as the President of Nalanda by the equally famous scholar Vasubandhu. Vasubandhu had as his disciple the equally famous Dignaga, an authority on Buddhist Logic, and a native of Kanchi who came to Nalanda on invitation to take part in disputation at a learned Conference which awarded to him the title of *Tarkapungava* for his victory in it.

Nalanda scholars were also examples of self-sacrifice in choosing to live as permanent exiles in foreign countries like China and Tibet to introduce to them Indian thought and culture. They equipped themselves for this sacred mission as linguists who could translate into Chinese and Tibetán the classics of Sanskrit and Pali religious literature. Among Nalanda scholars thus working in China may be mentioned Kumarajiva and Paramartha, the translator of the *Life* of Vasubandhu (of 5th Century A.D.), Subhakara Simha (of 8th Century) and Dharma Deva who during 40 years (A.D. 960-1000) translated into Chinese as many as 118 Buddhist texts!

The Tibetan *Tripitaka* mentions the contributions made by the scholars and books of Nalanda to the culture and civilization of Tibet. The works of Arya Deva, Ṣilabhadra, or Dharmapala were translated into Tibetan. Religious thinkers like Santarakshita (c. 749 A.D.), Padmasambhava (who went to Tibet in A.D. 747) or Atisa Dipankara Srijnana of Pundravardhana settled down in Tibet in the service of a sacred cause, and have been canonised by its devoted people. It was these scholars who helped to build up a Greater India in Asia. [Taranath's *History of Buddhism in India*].

We may now give an account of the material equipment of the University. It accommodated its vast population of about 15,000 in 7 monasteries and 8 halls of several storeys, with "their upper rooms towering above the clouds like pointed hill-tops," as described by the Chinese pilgrim.

The University was also equipped with an adequate Library located in a separate area aptly called *Dharmaganja*, 'the Mart of Piety' or 'Abode of Religion,' and housed in three buildings appropriately designated as *Ratnasagara*, *Ratnodadhi*, and *Ratnaranjaka*, 'Oceans of Gems of Learning.' *Ratnaranjaka* was probably the Library of Fine Arts or Belles-Letters, while the two others were libraries of Philosophy and Religion. *Ratnasagara* was a big library of 9 storeys.

An inscription of the Maukhari King Yasovarmmadeva (729-43 A.D.) describes how Nalanda was a vast collection of hostels or *Viharas* (*Viharavali*), "the rows of whose summits (*sikhara-sreni*) kissed the clouds (*ambudhara-valehi*)."

The University had its own Seal to testify to its corporate character. It bore the inscription: *Sri-Nalanda-Mahavihariya-Arya-Bhikshu-Sanghasya*, 'Of the Sangha or Community of venerable Monks in charge of the Holy and central Monastery of Nalanda.' The individual affiliated colleges called *Viharas* had also their own seals: e.g., the Baladitya college (*Gandhakuti* or *Kudi*) of Nalanda (*Sri-Nalandayam*).

A notable feature of Nalanda was its democratic management in several matters. It assigned to its student democracy its appropriate share in administration. They were in charge of residentical arrangements and the annual allotment of rooms to boarders. Seniors trusted their Juniors to look after their physical needs. Discipline was left to them as their own concern. They were to judge of cases of offences against the brotherhood, and could expel the offenders. The result of this democratic management was that the problems of indiscipline among students did not trouble the University, so that, as recorded by Yuan Chwang, "there did not occur a single case of any guilty rebellion against the Institution." Besides, even the budget of the University was passed by "the General body of the Monks" including teachers and students, who in this case were grown-ups as post-graduate students. Such mature students, indeed, made the case for their democratic association with the administration of the University.

It is again to be noted that Nalanda was not only a centre of the study of humanities, of Religion and Philosophy, of spiritual life and practice of Yoga of which its President was a master. It was also a centre of practical education and business training in the arts and crafts of the times described as *Silpasthana-vidya*, including medical education. The economy of the times centred mainly round Agriculture and Dairy-farming which had to be organised efficiently by the University for its own maintenance for which grants of land were made in those days, instead of monetary grants. Thus Emperor Harsha made a grant of 100 villages with their revenues to Nalanda in the time of Yuan Chwang (*Life of Yuan Chwang*, p. 112), while, in the time of I-tsing, the endowment increased to "more than 200 villages." The University had to find the means of its maintenance out of these lands donated to it by utilising them for purposes of efficient and profitable cultivation of food crops and dairy-farming. It had to depend upon its own farms for the daily supply of food for its populous colony. According to the Chinese pilgrim's estimate, the University's daily requirement of food which was carted from its paddy-fields and dairy-farms amounted to "several hundred *piculs* of ordinary rice, and several hundred *cotties* in weight of butter and milk." One picul=133 lbs.=66½ seers=about 1¾ maunds, while one cotty=150 lbs.=75 seers=about 2 maunds. Thus the University had to feed its own population from the produce of its own farms with rice and protective foods like milk, and its products like butter, constituting a most nutritive diet for them.

The University had also to depend upon itself for the supply of clothing for its alumni, according to established educational tradition as recorded in canonical Buddhist texts. It was felt that the Monks in residence "were ill at ease without the practice of some handicraft." Every monk was thus enjoined to toil, spin and weave. He was allowed "the use of a loom, and of shutters, strings, tickets and all the apparatus belonging to a loom". The monks had to make their own robes and keep them in fit condition with the help of all necessary weaving appliances (*Chullavagga*, V. II, V. 28). It is to be noted that the student was allowed the uniform of a scanty and simplified triple clothing (*Chivara*) made up of three parts, the upper garment to be untailored and worn as a wrapper, the lower garment reaching from waist to foot (the *dhoti*), and a towel. Thus spinning yarn and weaving cloth out of it was a compulsory handicraft to be plied by every monk as a part of his education.

The affairs of the University were administered by an adequate executive staff which, according to I-tsing, included the following officers viz., (1) *Viharapala*, the Principal of the *Vihara*, whose duty was "to enforce the rules, regulate admission, and report its affairs to the Assembly of Monks"; (2) *Viharasvami*, the Master of the College; (3) the Keeper of the University's seals, records, and effects (like modern Registrar); and (4) *Karmadana*, the Superintendent of Hostels. The Buddhist canonical texts mention various other officers charged with the administration of the *Vihara*, such as officers to apportion (1) Rooms, (2) Rations, (3) Robes, together with *Aramikas* in charge of the university's grounds and campus, and overseers or *Navakammikas* to supervise the construction and repairs of buildings.

As already stated, the University included in its Courses of Study the arts and crafts of the country described as *Silpasthanavidya* as a compulsory subject, besides *Chikitsa-vidya*, or medicine.

This training in arts and crafts led to the development of a regular School of Art at Nalanda, producing images and sculptures in stone, metal or bronze, inspired by the prevailing religions of the times, Mahayana and its later developments known as Tantrayana, Vajrayana and Kalachakrayana. Yuan Chwang saw the worship at Nalanda of the deities, Tara, Buddha, and Bodhisattva, and I-tsing, Hariti.

Nalanda fashioned a variety of images in stone and bronze, images of the Buddha, Bodhisattvas like Manjusri and Avalokitesvara, of female deities like Hariti, Tara, Prajnaparamita or Vasudhara; images of Tantrika deities like Trailokyavijaya, Heruka, Marichi, Vajrapani and the divine Bodhisattva; and images of Brahminical deities, Vishnu, Siva, Ganesa, Surya, Durga and the like.

I-tsing says that "the beauty of these marvellous sculptured images touches the limit in the art of ornamentation".

Special notice is due to the bronzes of Nalanda touching the height of art under its masters, father and son, named Dhiman and Bitpál who were natives of Varendra (North Bengal). This art flourished in the time of the Pala Kings, Dharmapala and Devapala (780-860 A.D.).

These bronzes depended upon progress in metallurgical processes and metal-casting testified to in the remnants of series of ovens found in the court-yards of the Nalanda monasteries.

CHAPTER XII

GREATER INDIA

An account has been given in a previous chapter of early Indian expansion up to the fourth century A.D., the time of Samudra Gupta. That process later developed into a regular colonial and cultural movement by which Indian thought gradually spread and penetrated into several countries in Asia, where it expressed itself in art and language, in monuments, inscriptions, and social institutions formed on Indian pattern. To all these countries as a whole Zimmer has aptly applied the designation "Indian Asia", and other scholars, "*Greater India*", while Sanskrit texts like the *Puranas* use the term *Dvipantara-Bharata*, 'India of the Islands', as distinguished from continental India or Indian mainland. It may be noted that the modern term Indonesia also connotes 'India of the islands' ("*nesia*" being the term for an island). These different countries of Asia which came under Indian influence were (1) Afghanistan, (2) Korea, (3) Mongolia, (4) Japan, (5) China, (6) Champa, (7) Cambodia, (8) Thailand, (9) Burma, (10) Malaya Peninsula and (11) Indonesia comprising within its limits approximately as many as 3,000 islands of which the prominent ones are Java, Sumatra, Borneo and Bali. The penetration of Indian thought into all these countries was achieved by the spread of Sanskrit through translations and adaptations of Sanskrit works along with local works. Translations of Sanskrit works are found in Mongolian, Manchurian, Korean, and Japanese. Sanskrit works lost in India have been preserved in Tibetan and Chinese translations.

This spread of Indian thought was due to its innate elasticity which accommodated within its comprehensive fold and assimilated to its synthetic system, diverse foreign elements, cults and creeds. This feature is indicated in a typical passage of the *Mahabharata* as a text of normal Hinduism. That passage [*Mbh.* XV., V. 13], for instance, allows Vedic ceremonies to such foreign peoples as "Yavanas, Kiratas Gandharas, Tusharas and Pahlavas, who were living in Aryan Kingdoms". It is this catholicity of outlook which indefinitely multiplied Indian societies in foreign countries, both on the Asiatic mainland, and overseas.

A few glimpses into this vast story of Greater India will now be given. Indian thought extended through Afganistan, and built up a noted centre of Buddhism in *Bamiyan* with its grottos shaped into temples, its colossal Buddhas 125 feet and 175 feet high cut out of rock, and its collection of Buddhist manuscripts.

We may next mention *Khotan* with its Gomati *Vihara* of which the monks composed their own canonical texts. Many Indian texts have been found in Khotan such as *Dhammapada* in Kharoshthi. There was also developed a special Khotan Sanskrit.

Kuchi is marked out by its *stupas* and temples in one of which was discovered the famous medical text known as the Bower manuscript.

At *Dandan Uilik* Sir Aurel Stein discovered "frescoes inscribed with Brahmi characters, objects of Buddhist worship, and leaves of paper covered with old Brahmi characters of Gupta type, with a page number 132."

Niya is famous for the find of 500 wooden inscribed tablets, "about two dozen Kharoshthi documents on leather in Prakrit," containing expressions like *Mahanuva Maharaya lihafi*="*Mahanubhava-Maharaja likhati.*" The wooden tablets are documents of business.

Bazaklik was another centre of Buddhism, with its hundreds of temples adorned with paintings of Buddhist monks whose names are written in Brahmi.

Tun-huang was famous for its "Thousand Buddha Stone Caves," its Library of Buddhist manuscripts in different languages, Chinese, Sanskrit, Tibetan, Khotanese, and the like, and its paintings dating from 4th century A.D.

These Central Asian antiquities represented both Buddhism and Brahminism.

The history of cultural contact between India and *China* is a long one continuing through centuries. Its result in the progress of Buddhism in China is thus summed up by Dr. F. W. Thomas: "The third century A.D. saw 180 monasteries with 3700 monks in China, with 13 Indian translators who rendered into Chinese 73 Indian works. The fourth century saw 17,068 temples and translation of 263 works by 27 translators. The sixth century saw 3000 Indians settled in China" (*Indianism and its expansion*, Calcutta, pp. 93, 94.)

Indian influence also crossed over the seas into the countries of *South-East Asia*, as already stated. It originated in the voyages of traders in ocean-going vessels carrying up to 600 passengers each. The trading centres became the centres of Indian influence and culture. There soon arose out of these several Indianised States overseas. "These spiritual colonies represented by Borobudur and Angkor Vat constitute India's greatest title to fame, her contribution to mankind" (Rene Grousset).

Burma across the Bay of Bengal felt the impact of Indian thought from first century A.D. Some of its places are named after those of the Mother Country such as Sri Kshetra, Suvarnabhumi (Thaton and Pegu), Utkaladesa (from Rangoon to Pegu), while the entire Mon kingdom of sixth century called itself Dvaravati. The third century saw in Burma more than a lac of Buddhist families, with thousands of monks. But Burma also shows monuments of other Hindu sects, Saivaism and Vaishnavism, besides Hinayana, Mahayana, and Tantrika Buddhism. Many Buddhist monuments were built by Aniruddha, while his son, Kyanzitha, built the Buddhist temple of Ananda, the pride of Pagan, and a masterpiece of Indian art.

Siam (Thailand) was made up of several States. Its first Hindu colony was called Dvaravati noted for its Indian sculptures. The State of Yunnan was called Gandhara while the term Kausambi was applied to the entire area between the Irawaddy and Salween. There were two other Thai States called Sukhodaya and Ayodhya, with their Buddhist monuments and Pali language.

Kambuja (which included Funan and Chan-la of the Chinese) began as a Hindu settlement founded by Brahmana Kaundinya and moulded by Hindu institutions such as study of Veda, Caste, Vaishnavism, Saivaism, with Temples of Hindu deities. Its part known as Fu-nan built up its famous city known as *Ankar Thom* (=Nagara-dhama). Its king Yasovardhana (889 A.D.), who was a Sanskritist and wrote a commentary on Patanjali's *Mahabhashya,* built temples, *asramas,* and *viharas,* while his successor Suryavarman II (1113-1145 A.D.) built the magnificent Vaishnava temple known as *Ankor Vat,* one of the wonders of the world, with its pyramids, towers, galleries, and sculptures showing characters of Indian epics, with the characteristic 'smile of Ankor.' "It is no exaggeration to say that every stone of Angkor Vat, and every building of this period, bear the stamp of perfection. Henceforth no further progress is possible." Hindu culture reached its acme under the next king Jayavarman II (1181 A.D.) who built a new Ankor Thom, with the Great Temple of *Bayon,* an example of art, and another huge temple, with an endowment of 3,400 villages, maintaining a school of 970 scholars taught by 434 teachers, and employing a menial staff of 66,625. The whole country was decorated with as many as 798 temples. It was equipped with Indian institutions called *Vipra-sala* (Home of Sages), *Arogya-sala* (Hospitals), *Satra* and *Vahnigriha* (temple of Agni). Its inscriptions mention such subjects of study as Vaiseshika, Nyaya-Samiksha, Arthasastra, works like Raghuvamsa, and those of the Prakrit author Gunadhya. Its king Sivasoma is stated to have gone to India to study as a direct pupil of "Bhagavat Sankara Himself at whose lotus feet bowed the heads of sages."

One monument of Ankor Vat bears the following significant inscription: "He (the ideal king) suffered from the ills of his subjects more than from his own, for it is the grief of the people that causes the grief of kings, and not their own grief" (*Angkor* by Groslier and Arthand; tr. by Smith).

Khmer greatness declined in 12th century. Its prosperity was destroyed by the cost of gigantic edifices while it was invaded by the Chams who destroyed Angkor in 1177 and the Thais became powerful neighbours.

The decline was checked for a time by Jayavarman VII (1181).

Champa (Annam). Its first Hindu king was Sri Mara of 2nd century A.D. His successor Bhadravarma ruled over its three provinces called Amaravati, Vijaya, and Panduranga, and built the Bhadresvara (Siva) temple at Mysore. It became the national temple of the Chams. The official language of the country was Sanskrit used in its more than 100 inscriptions. Saivism was the popular religion. There were also temples of Hindu deities like Vishnu, Rama, Krishna, Brahma and Sakti, together with such minor deities as Ganesha, Kartika, Lakshmi, Garuda, Yama, Chandra, Surya, Sarasvati and Nandi. Along with Hinduism flourished Buddhism which had its centre in Dong Duong.

The art of Champa takes after that of Mamallapuram.

Malaya. Its Sanskrit inscriptions of 4th century A.D. point to Hindu colonies of Kankasuka and Tamralinga with its capital Ligor. Brahminical and Buddhist antiquities have been found at sites known as Perak and Kedah. At Kedah has been found an inscription mentioning a great Captain of Navigation (*Mahanavika*) named Buddhagupta who hailed from Rangamati of Murshedabad District in West Bengal. The king named Pan-Pan who ruled in northern Kanakasuka (A.D. 424-53) sent an embassy of Brahmins to China. These came from India. .

Suvarnadvipa (or *Dvipanlara Bharala*=modern Indonesia). This region comprised the islands of the Indian Archipelago numbering about 3,000 of which the more famous are Java, Sumatra, Borneo, and Bali. Both Hinduism and Buddhism spread to these islands.

Sumatra (Sri-Vijaya). This Hindu colony was founded in the fourth century A.D. I-tsing in the seventh century found Buddhism flourishing here by its intercourse with India by her mercantile marine.

Borneo. A striking proof of Hinduism in this island is its inscriptions written in Pallava-Grantha characters of 4th century A.D. on seven *Yupas* of stone to record the celebration by King Mulavarman of a *Bahusuvarnaka Yajna.*

Bali. It is a centre of Hinduism to this day. Its people perform the Hindu ceremonies (*Samskaras*) of domestic life and worship deities like Siva, Brahma, Ganesha, Skanda, and Mahakala. It has three temples of Varuna.

Java. Both Hinduism and Buddhism spread to Java, as seen in its many monuments inspired by Indian Art and containing sculptures some of which excel its quality and rank as its best examples. A group of Hindu temples (*Chandis*) such as those of Bhima and Arjuna is found in Central Java. There are also the Buddhist *Chandis* of Kalasam, Mendut, and Pawon, attaining their culmination in the stupendous *Chandi* or *Stupa* of Borobudur showing 1,400 sculptures and 400 statues of the Buddha. The sculptures illustrate events of the Buddha's life, and previous lives as narrated in the *Jatakas*. There are also portraits of

Dhyani Buddhas like Amitabha and of *Bodhisattvas* like Maitreya speaking to a person supposed to be Asanga to whom he is said to have revealed some Buddhist texts. The sculptures of the *Stupa* appear like translations in stone of the texts of Mahayana. An inscription dated 842 A.D. at its base labels the *Stupa* as *Bhumisambhara* and another dated 824. A.D. mentions the Sailendra king Samaratunga as its builder.

There are also a few other Buddhist temples such as (i) *Sewee* (thousand temples) surrounded by a group of 246 smaller temples in four rows and (2) *Plavson* with artistic images of Tara and Pādmapani.

As already stated, Java is also known for its Hindu temples such as (1) Chandi Bayon near Borobudur, containing artistic figures of Vishnu, Siva, Brahma, Ganesa and Agastya; (2) Chandi Loro Janggrang at Prambanam (=Brahmavanam), a huge structural complex of a Siva temple, with its adjunct of 156 smaller temples. Within itself it contains separate shrines of Siva, Vishnu and Brahma, besides images of these, together with Durga-Mahishamardini and Vishnu Seshasayi. There are also sculptures depicting scenes from *Ramayana* and of Krishna's life which are comparable to the Borobudur portraiture of the events of the Buddha's life. On the whole, the Prambanam relics show a higher artistic standard than those of Borobudur in the opinion of Dr. A. K. Coomaraswamy.

Tibet. The story of Greater India will not be complete without a reference to the prominent place filled in it to this day by one of India's neighbours, Tibet. It is surprising that Tibetan language is perhaps the only non-Indian language which is fundamentally linked with Sanskrit. Tibet had its own native literature but it was handed down orally.

Tibetan tradition seeks to relate Tibetan culture to India, and traces its origins in India, a hero of *Mahabharata* War, and also other sources like the holy Sakya clan, Lichchhavis, and royal families of Magadha, Kosala and Vatsa.

Tibet first emerges into history under King Son-tsan-gampo (6th-7th century A.D.). He sent to Kashmir his minister Thon-mi, who studied there Grammar under Devavidya-simha, invented the Tibetan alphabet, and made of Tibetan a literary language into which could be translated Buddhist literature. The introduction of Buddhism into Tibet was also influenced by his two queens a Chinese and a Nepali.

Buddhism was firmly established in Tibet under King Tri-son de tsan of 8th century A.D. with the help of Indian scholars Santarakshita (author of treatises like *Tattvasam-graha*) and his disciple Kamalasila, followed by the great saint Padmasambhava whose services to Tibetan Buddhism are celebrated in many legends and epics in Tibet. The *Vinaya* (*Mulasarvastivadi*) was now established, Tibetan youths were now being trained as monks, and Indian texts were translated into Tibetan, leading to the transformation of Tibetan Buddhism from its Chinese form to Indian, under the influence of Kamalasila and his discourses on *Madhya-mika* and *Vijnanavada* philosophy and practice. This *Madhyamika* tradition is the foundation of the yellow sect of which the Dalai Lama is the leader.

Buddhism found a most zealous devotee in King Ral-pa-chan of 9th century A.D. But it suffered an eclipse under King Lan-dar-ma who was a persecutor of Buddhism.

Buddhism, however, after some time regained its position under the Bengali scholar Atisa Dipankara Srijnana of Varendra, who came on invitation in 1042 A.D. to Tibet where he died in 1054. Atisa founded in Tibet the most famous of its schools from which descended her "Yellow Sect" to which belongs the Dalai Lama, as already stated. Then followed an era of active intercourse between India and Tibet through visits of scholars. This cultural inter-course received a set-back under Moslem invasions destroying India's *Viharas* and their libraries, but this only resulted in a larger movement of Indian scholars to Tibet as refugees, while the visit of Tibetan scholars to India was not completely stopped. Indeed, owing to the work of theso great scholars, Indian and Tibetan, Buddhism in all its doctrines and schools was firmly planted in Tibet which thereby became the unsurpassed repository of Buddhist discipline, learning and culture. Thus the basis of Tibetan spiritual and intellectual culture is the fully developed form of Buddhism brought from India.

CHAPTER XIII

UNITY

THE concepion of India's inherent unity has been developed through the ages on the basis of undivided India stretching from Kashmir to Cape Comorin as a single country. Its unity is writ large on its map. Mountain-guarded in the north, and sea-girt in the south, India has been planned by Nature as an indisputable geographical unit sharply isolated from the world outside by natural boundaries forming formidable barriers to intercourse with foreign countries. The north is protected by the Himalayas, a double wall of about 1,600 miles in length and of an average width of 50 miles. At the eastern end, there is a barrier of Patkoi, Naga, and Lushai hills, along with dense forests. Towards the north-west, the barrier of the Himalayas is continued by the Karakoram range, and Hindukush, and, further south, by Sufed Khoh, Sulaiman, and Kirthar hills, separating India from Afghanistan and Baluchistan.

India's geography has moulded her history which is more a product of isolation than of intercourse with the outside world or foreign influence.

On the other hand, the very vastness of her area has itself produced a variety which militates against her unity. The variety is both physical and cultural. Physically, India appears as an epitome of the world in the variety of her natural products, flora and fauna, and the assemblage within her limits of conditions distributed among its different countries.

Again, her social variety is equally pronounced. She has as many as 179 languages and 545 dialects, though the number of languages that count for their literature is reduced to 15. These are Tamil and Telugu, Kanarese and Malayalam in the South, and in the North, Hindi, Gujerati, Marathi, Bengali, Oriya, and Assamese. There are in addition several tribal languages of Austric and Tibeto-Chinese families of speech known as Munda, though these are spoken by only 2% of India's population.

Side by side with this linguistic variety operates the unifying influence of Sanskrit, the mother of most of the Indian vernaculars. As has been well pointed out by Monier Williams (*Hinduism*, p. 18), "India, though it has more than 500 spoken dialects, has only one sacred language and only one sacred literature, accepted and revered by all adherents of Hinduism alike, however diverse in race, dialect, rank, and creed. That language is Sanskrit and that Literature is Sanskrit Literature, the only repository of *Veda* or knowledge in its widest sense; the only vehicle of Hindu theology, philosophy, law and mythology; the only mirror in which all the creeds, opinions, customs and usages of the Hindus are faithfully reflected; and, if we may be allowed a fourth metaphor, the only quarry whence the requisite material may be obtained for improving the vernaculars, or for expressing important religious and scientific ideas."

India has also been the abode of the principal religions of the world, Hinduism, Islam, Christianity, Jainism and Buddhism. Hinduism is, however, a unifying factor as the religion of the majority, of over 250 millions of people whose spiritual requirements are met by a multiplicity of cults and creeds comprehended within its synthetic system and flexible structure.

Again, India's social composition represents the main racial types of mankind, the Negritos found in Kerala, the tribal proto-Australoids, the Mediterraneans represented in Brahmins of different regions, the Brachy-cephals of Gujarat, the Dinaric type of Bengal and Orissa, and the Nordic type of Panjab, Rajasthan, Maharashtra, and also Bengal.

There is, however, a fundamental cultural unity behind all this diversity. The fathers of India's civilisation were alive to the primary need of training the people's mind in the conception of what constitutes their Motherland to whom is due their national homage. They formulated prayers calling up the physical form and visible image of Mother India for meditation and worship. One prayer defines India as the land of seven sacred rivers covering between them a large part of the country from north to south. Millions of devout Hindus of different parts of the country take their bath on the same festival day in their sacred waters to the utterance of a common purificatory prayer which unites them in spirit as brethren of the same faith. These rivers are: Ganga, Yamuna, Godavari, Sarasvaṭi, Narmada, Sindhu (Indus) and Kaveri. The prayer addressed to them is: "Come ye and impart thy collective purity to the water I am offering for worship!"

Another prayer calls up the image of Mother India as the land of seven sacred cities which a devotee should visit on pilgrimage as an aid to salvation by capturing the religious spirit with which they are charged by their association with the principal Deities of Hinduism. These are Ayodhya, the city of Rama, Mathura of Krishna, Maya (Hardwar) of Goddess Ganga, Kasi of Siva, Kanchi dedicated to both Siva and Vishnu, Avanti of Mahakala, and Dvaraka of Krishna-Balarama.

"And in the story of Sati, the perfect wife, who can miss the significance of the 52 places (*pithas*) in which the fragments of her smitten body fell? And one finger fell in Calcutta and that is still the Kalighat. And the tongue fell at Kangra (Jwalamukhi) in the north Panjab and appears to this day as licking tongues of fire, from underneath the ground. And the left hand fell at Banaras, which is for ever Annapurna, the Giver-of-bread!" (Sister Nivedita in her *Web of Indian Life*).

Indeed, the different sects of Hinduism are at one in one fundamental point. They vie with one another in covering the country with a network of their respective holy places, which it is obligatory for their followers to visit. It is ultimately the Hindu mode of worshipping the country. Such pilgrimage imparts to the devotee an extended geographical horizon and a living consciousness of the dimensions (the *Viratdeha*) of their great country. Thus sectarianism is ultimately an education in nationalism.

Thus the institution of pilgrimage is undeniably a most powerful instrument of mass education in nationalism and patriotism. It develops in the people the geographical sense which enables them to feel the immensity of their mother-country pulsating with a common life from end to end in its vast area. Pilgrimage has also made travelling a national habit in India in spite of its hardships in the days of pre-mechanical transport. But its very difficulties added to its educative value in giving to travellers a deeper knowledge of the country than is possible to modern globe-trotters or flying visitors. At the same time, the severities of old-world travelling were very much mitigated by the breaks of the pilgrims' progress at holy halting places at short intervals such as myriads of village temples on its routes. This specifically Hindu institution of pilgrimage by promoting this popular habit of travelling through the country greatly helped in the spread of education among the masses. Learned men joined the pilgrims and delivered discourses in the countryside on religion and philosophy, and also on its local problems which they helped to solve. These travelling scholars who wandered through the country in their zeal for carrying their learning to the people at large by means of public lectures are aptly called *Charakas* in the Upanishads. It was these scholars and their social mission of self-sacrifice and service to the people that achieved the spread of learning and religion all over the country from north to south, and east to west. The *Veda* originating in the north in the land of the Seven Rivers (*saptasindhavah*) gradually spread to all parts of the country up to the south where it at once took root. The south became the home of Vedic learning. The Veda was on the lips of the learned in every part of India, and especially at its places of pilgrimage. And yet learning spread in those days without the help of the modern methods of communication and publicity. It was literally carried from mouth to mouth, from teacher to pupil, in a system of oral tradition. It was not locked up in dead manuscripts. The teachers were the living libraries of those days in ancient India. The teachers and texts moved together through the country, bringing their store of knowledge to its centres of learning at the centres of pilgrimage, which thus operated as a most potent instrument of popular education in patriotism and nationalism, in religion and politics.

The geographical conception of the identity and individuality of the country in all its vastness and variety led to the conception of its political unification under one sovereignty. The ideal of one sovereign ruling the entire country up to its limits is as old as the *Vedas*. It was expressed in a variety of terms stated together in the *Aitareya Brahmana*, terms like *Rajadhiraja* or *Samrat* (king of kings) or *Ekarat*. The title of *Samrat* was applied to the kings of eastern India (*prachyam disi*) (in anticipation, perhaps, of Magadhan imperialism). The term *Ekarat* is more significant as applying to 'the king ruling over the whole country (*prithvi*) up to the sea as its limit' (*samudraparyantaya Ekaraditi*). The term is explained by Sayana to mean 'the sole sovereign without a rival' (*nihsapatno mukhyo raja*), 'the king of eastern peoples' (*pran vis'ampatih ekarat tvam*). This status is achieved by power [*varchasa* (*balena saha*) *udihi* (*uditah prakhyato bhava*)]. The *Satapatha Brahmana* prays for the king's rule over 'an extended territory' (*mahato janarajyaya*).

Besides these terms, the Vedic texts tell of ceremonies to celebrate the king's attainment of the status of an emperor, ceremonies like the *Vajapeya*, *Rajasuya*, *Asvamedha* and *Aindra-Mahabhisheka*, of which the prayer prescribed is for 'the attainment of status superior to that of all kings as a *Sarvabhauma*, lord of whole earth.'

'But the books are not content with the mere prescription of ceremonies in celebration of imperial inaugurations. They give lists of great kings who actually achieved the status of imperial sovereignty. Such a typical king of kings was Bharata Daushmanti "the height of whose achievements was as inaccessible as the heavens to human hands."

The political ideal held up before the king is thus described in the *Aitareya Brahmana* (VIII 4, 1): "Monarchy at its highest should have an empire extending right up to natural boundaries; it should be territorially all-embracing, up to the very ends uninterrupted, and should constitute and establish one State and administration in the land up to the seas." Thus the conception of India, both as a geographical and political unit, has not been foreign to the consciousness of its people.

But apart from these pre-historic names of great kings dictated by a prevailing political conception, and indicative of some degree of realism in the background, history also records the names of some kings who were able to utilise the national factor and asset of India's geographical unity to achieve the difficult task of the political unification of a country as vast as a continent. These were kings like Chandragupta Maurya (c. 323-299 B.C.) and his grandson, the famous Asoka (274-235 B.C.) who established their paramount sovereignty over a Greater India which extended from the borders of Persia up to Southern India and even beyond up to Tamraparni (Ceylon), whither Asoka despatched his son and daughter to work as missionaries in permanent exile, for introducing to that foreign country Indian thought and Buddhism.

This remarkable process of the expansion of India is itself the product of an awakened national consciousness and awareness of her intrinsic unity and inherent individuality.

CHAPTER XIV

LINGUISTIC AND LITERARY LEGACY

Variety of Languages. India is possessed of a rich linguistic legacy derived from several families of speech, Indo-Aryan, Dravidian, Austric, and Tibeto-Chinese prevailing in the country. The *Linguistic Survey of India* computes the living languages of India at as many as 179, and dialects at 544. Of the 179 languages, 116 belong to Tibeto-Chinese family of speech, and are spoken only by a small number, less than 1% of India's population. The tribal languages derive from Austric and Tibeto-Chinese families of speech. The Austric languages are known as Munda. The languages that count for culture and learning are only 15 and are both Aryan and Dravidian. The Dravidian languages are four viz., Tamil, Telugu, Kanarese and Malayalam. Indo-Aryan is represented by a number of Aryan languages, each with its own literature, such as Hindi, Gujarati, Marathi, Bengali, Oriya and Assamese.

The early linguistic history of India is the history of the spread of the Indo-Aryan language of Sanskrit which also influenced the Dravidian languages chiefly in vocabulary, as these had their own lines of internal development. But Sanskrit itself could not escape dialectical variety in its process of expansion from the Indus to the borders of Bengal, and in adaptation to popular speech. In fact, Vedic Sanskrit co-existed with the popular speech of the day. It was recognised by the Buddha who used it for carrying his new religion to the masses. The first emergence of the vernacular is found in the Edicts of Asoka giving it official recognition. It was a vernacular descended from the Vedic dialect and prevailing parallel with Sanskrit as the vehicle of Jainism and Buddhism under the name of Prakrit. The oldest Prakrit is called Pali. The Prakrit used in the Jain canon is known as Ardhamagadhi. There was in time the evolution of literary Prakrits, learned and artificial like Sanskrit, and also of Apabhramsas or degenerate popular dialects which also later attained a literary form. After about 300 A.D. Prakrit fell into disuse in official and monumental documents.

Predominance of Sanskrit. Turning now to the main linguistic heritage of India in Sanskrit, aptly described as the mother of the regional languages of India, we may consider it in its literary aspect. Sanskrit literature is one of the greatest contributions India has made to the culture of mankind. It is remarkable for its longevity, vastness of volume, and variety of form and style. The *Rigveda* is the root of the tree of knowledge, with its many offshoots and branches in different sects and schools growing out of it through the ages. It marks at once the dawn and zenith of thought. For instance, its most popular hymn, the Gayatri Mantram, contains the earliest conception of God as the thinking principle in man (*dhi*). It also describes how God created the Universe by sacrificing His cosmic body (*virat deha*) as its material, and sustaining it by breathing life into it. Like God, man made after God's image should also find his *dharma*, his highest duty, in self-sacrifice for his own little system. Indeed, the essence of the religion of the *Rigveda* is the worship of the One in the Many as described in so many hymns.

Samghas. The *Rigveda* also mentions *Samghas* or learned assemblies of comrades (*sakha*) in culture, whose discussions refined popular language (*Vacham laukikim*) into Vedic Sanskrit, like "getting groats through a sieve." Popular speech could not serve like Vedic Sanskrit as the vehicle of highest thought but only for purposes of secular life in the field or factory for people "plying the plough or the loom."

Rigveda. The *Rigveda* in its present form is a collection (*samhita*) of select hymns numbering 1017 out of a mass accumulated through the ages. "Centuries must have elapsed between the composition of the earliest hymns and the completion of the *Samhita* of the Rigveda" (Winternitz).

Vedic Samhitas. The *Rigveda* was followed by three other Vedic *Samhitas* called *Sama, Yajuh* and *Atharva*. The *Samaveda* is a selection of Rigvedic hymns for purposes of chanting. The *Yajurveda* contains the formulae and prayers to be used by the *Adhvaryu* (priest) for performance of worship. It was in both prose and verse. The *Atharvaveda* is a book of 131 hymns containing some amount of secular matter, such as diseases, economic prosperity, social harmony, marriage and love, and royalty.

Brahmanas. The Vedic *Samhitas* were followed by prose works known as the *Brahmanas, Aranyakas,* and *Upanishads*. The *Brahmanas* deal with rituals adumbrated in the *Karma-kanda* of the *Rigveda*. The *Aranyakas* or 'Books of the Woods' are so called because they contain mystical and subtle truths which are to be thought out in the silence and solitude of the forests. They arise out of the *Upasana-Kanda* of the *Rigveda*. The *Upanishads* arise out of its *Jnana-Kanda* and give exposition of highest knowledge and philosophy.

Vedangas. Vedic Literature was completed by its six Supplements known as *Vedangas* which were technical studies concerning *Siksha* (phonetics), *Kalpa* (ritual), *Chhanda* (metre) *Nirukta* (etymology), *Vyakarana* (grammar) any *Jyotish* (astronomy). These works are the precursors of the special literature of *Sutras* or aphorisms based on the ideal literary style expressing the maximum of sense in the minimum of words. They proved very valuable as store-houses of knowledge on topics like rituals, public and domestic, and law (*Kalpa-grihya-dharma-sutras*). Their brevity and name are perhaps explained by the fact that they served as aids to memory in ancient India where writing was late in coming.

as it was banned by the Veda. The best example of *Sutra* literature is the *Ashtadhyayi* of Panini, 'a most singular triumph of Indian intellect.'

The Epics. Outside priestly studies there were works of fiction (*akhyana*), poetry and drama, narrative (*purana* and *itihasa*), *Narasamsa-gathas* in praise of heroes and *Vakovakya* or dialogues, culminating in the two great Epics, the *Ramayana* and *Mahabharata.* Their political background is that of the multiplicity of kingdoms prior to Nanda-Maurya Empire and even Buddhism of 6th Century B.C.

The *Ramayana* is more Vedic than *Mahabharata,* in the part played in it by the Ikshvakus, a Vedic people, and Vedic Rishis like Vasishtha, Vishvamitra and Gautama, and the philosopher-king Janaka of Videha, showing that eastern India was already Aryanised. The *Ramayana* is also supposed to be the story of the spread of Aryan culture towards the South up to Ceylon.

The *Mahabharata* is a composite work of 100,000 *slokas* containing contributions of different authors and periods. Panini's grammar mentions Vasudeva and Arjuna as already deified. It is dated between 750 B.C. (Bhandarkar) and 500 B.C. (Macdonell). The *Ramayana* as the work of a single author described as *Adikavi,* and presenting ideal characters, has become a more popular and sacred work than the other Epic.

Pali. The Pali canon comprised the *Tipitaka,* was first constituted under Asoka and was made up of (1) *Vinaya,* (2) *Suttas,* sermons, in five collections including *Dhammapada, Thera*-and Theri-*gatha;* also the *Jataka* of 550 stories of Buddha's previous lives and (3) *Abhidhamma* or higher religion.

Hinayana had Pali as its vehicle. It also used Sanskrit, as in *Dharmapada* and *Mahavastu, Lalita-vistara* and *Buddha-charita* of Asvaghosha, and *Avadanas,* e.g. *Divyavadana.*

Mahayana also used Sanskrit as its vehicle, as in *Sad-dharma-pundarika.* It was systematised by Brahmin Nag-arjuna in about 200 A.D. and Brahmin Asanga (300-350 A.D.) of Peshawar, who introduced *Yoga* into Mahayana. Buddhist Tantra works were also in Sanskrit.

Jain Canon. Jainism used the Prakrit called Ardha-magadhi. They call their sacred books as *Siddhanta* or *Agama.* An important part of their canon is the twelve *Angas.* There is a large non-canonical literature of com-mentaries e.g. those of Bhadrabahu of 600 verses, of Santisuri and Devendragani.

The Jains had also collections of stories called *Katha-Kosa* and special poems called *Charitras* and *Pravandhas,* e.g. Hemachandra's *Trishashti-salaka-purusha-charitra* with Appendix called *Parisishta-parvan.* Hemachandra (born 1089 A.D.) was an encyclopaedic scholar who wrote on grammar, lexicography, poetics, and prosody. He was also the author of a poem called *Yogasastra.*

Jainism had also a large religious literature in Sanskrit. Haribhadra wrote the philosophical work *Shaddarsana-samuchchaya.* They also wrote in Sanskrit on grammar and astronomy, and also literature. They thus occupy an im-portant place in the history of Indian learning and civilisa-tion.

Puranas. Allied to the Epics are the *Puranas,* 18 in num-ber, of which the *Bhagavata Purana* is the most important. *Vishnupurana* is also noteworthy for its historical material mentioning the succeeding dynasties of kings and their periods of reign, offering valueable chronological data.

Stories. There was a considerable literature of stories re-presented in *Panchatantra; Brihatkatha* collection of stories by Gunadhya in Paisachi, with Sanskrit recensions; Kshemen-dra's *Brihatkatha-manjari;* and Somadeva's *Kathasarit-sagara,* in Kashmiri and Nepali.

Prose romances are represented in Dandins *Dasakumara-crita*, *Vasavadatta* of Subandhu, and Bana's *Kadambari* d *Harshacharita*.

Other types of Literature. There was a continuous develop-ent of Sanskrit literature in different types and forms which ay be distinguished as epic, lyric, dramatic, didactic, narra-ve, and scientific. We have already dealt with some of these ke the epic, didactic, and narrative. But the strong point of anskrit literature lies in the dramatic and lyric. As the *Iahabharata* inspired the *Puranas*, the *Ramayana* is the nodel of a number of court epics designated as *Kavyas* be-onging to the period 400-1100 A.D. The earliest example may be taken to be *Buddha-charita* of Asvaghosa of about 2nd Century A.D.

Poetry. Next, we may refer to the greatest poet of India, Kalidasa, who is generally taken to be of the 5th Century A.D. though there is a view that he might have lived in the time of the Sunga King Pushyamitra in the light of his drama called *Malavikagnimitra*. His two court epics are *Raghu-vamsa* aud *Kumarasambhava*.

Then followed *Kiratarjuniya* by Bharavi of about 6th century A.D.: *Bhatti-Kavya* of Bhartrihari who died in 651 A.D., relating the life of Rama in a manner designed to illustrate the rules of Sanskrit grammar; *Sisupala-vadha* by Magha of 7th century A.D.; *Nalodaya* noted for its lite-rary innovations of metre and rhyme as seen in later works like *Gīta-govinda* and *Moha-mudgara;* culminating in the artificial style of *Raghavapandaviya* by poet Kaviraja of about 800 A.D.

Lyrical poetry is best represented in the *Meghaduta* of Kalidasa, describing the message sent by an exile in Central India to his wife on the Himalayas by a cloud moving north-ward. Next is *Ritusamhara* attributed for its quality to Kalidasa, showing his love of Nature. It is, however, not known to later works on poetics.

Among other examples of lyrical poetry may be mentioned the *Sringara-sataka* of Bhartrihari (7th Century A.D.)

Drama. Sanskrit literature is also noted for dramatic works. The origin of drama may be seen in some hymns of the *Rig-veda* taking the form of a dialogue. Panini knows of *Natas* or dancers, and of *Nata-sutras*, handbooks for dancers. The Nata-sutras formed the basis of the classical and comprehensive work of Indian Drama, the *Natya-sastra* of Bharata (c. 200 B.C.) It inspired later dramatic literature of which the best example is *Dasa-rupa* (ten kinds of drama) by Dhananjaya of 10th Century A.D.

An early drama was *Sariputra-prakarana* of Asvaghosha, teacher of King Kanishka I.

These are about a dozen examples of good drama produced between *c.* 200-800 A.D. First come the dramas of Bhasa mentioned by Kalidasa in his *Malavikagnimitra* as a poet whose fame he cannot rival. He is also mentioned as having achieved fame by his plays (*nataka*) by Bana in his *Harshacharita*. Rajasekhara (*c.* 1000 A.D.) mentions *Svapna Vasavadatta* as a work of Bhasa. His existence is supposed to be proved by the discovery of 13 plays including *Svapna Vasavadatta*. Conclusions about Bhasa and his plays are still controversial.

The two greatest Sanskrit play-wrights were Kalidasa and Bhavabhuti. Kalidasa is the author of *Sakuntala*, which is made famous by the praise of Goethe, of *Vikramorvasiyam* and of *Malavikagnimitra*.

Bhavabhuti (*c.* 8th century), a Brahmin of Vidarbha (Berar) wrote *Malati-madhava* and *Uttara-ramacharita*.

Next comes Bhatta-Narayana (who lived before 800 A.D.), author of *Venisamhara* connected with Krishna cult.

Visakhadatta was the author of the historical play called *Mudrarakshasa*.

About 900 A.D. lived Rajasekhara known for his artificial metres and his two plays, *Balaramayana* and *Balabharata.*

Rajasekhara showed his mettle as a linguist by writing in Prakrit the famous comedy called *Karpura-manjari.*

A remarkable dramatic piece is *Prabodha Chandrodaya* of Krishnamisra (*c.* 1100 A.D.).

We may also mention a dramatic work of high quality marked by much vigour, life, action, and delineation of character, the *Mrichchhakatika* of Sudraka.

Harsha is a unique example in the annals of kingship of proficiency as a dramatist, who is remembered as the author of *Ratnavali, Priyadarsika,* and *Nagananda.*

Technical Literature. There was a considerable development of technical literature as described below.

Grammar. It was cultivated as the Science of Sciences and constitutes "India's greatest contribution to science and western philology" (Macdonell). India developed "a grammatical system so accurate and complete as to be unparalleled in any other country".

The beginnings of grammar were made in the linguistic study of Vedic hymns and in Sakalya's Pada text of the *Rigveda* based on grammatical analysis, in the works known as *Pratisakhyas* and *Sikshas,* and in Yaska's *Nirukta* implying a considerable grammatical development attaining its culmination in the *Sabdanusasana* of Panini, his work known as *Ashtadhyayi.*

Panini lived between 750 B.C. (Bhandarkar) and 500 B.C. (Macdonell) His work is based on the usages of Vedic literature and not classical Sanskrit which was, however, the basis of the works of his successors, Katyayana (*c.* 250 B.C.) in his *Varttikas,* and Patanjali (c. 150 B.C.) in his *Mahabhashya.* Panini had both commentaries like the *Kasika-Vritti* (c. 662 A.D.) and a popularised version like *Siddhan-*

Kaumudi of Bhattoji-dikshita (1025 A.D.) abridged in *Laghu-Kaumudi* of Varadaraja, and *Ganaratna-mahodadhi* by *Vardhamana* (1140 A.D.).

The philosophy of grammar is dealt with by Bhartrihari (651 A.D.) in his *Vakyapadiya*.

Among other works of grammar may be mentioned *Chandra-Vyakarana* of Chandragomin followed in Kashmir, Nepal, Tibet and Ceylon; *Sakatayana Vyakarana* of 9th century A.D. improved upon by the work of Hemachandra; and *Mugdha-bodha* of Bopadeva, which offers a new system prevalent in Bengal.

Prakrit had its own grammar modelled on Panini, e.g., *Prakrita-prakasa* of Vararuchi (C 650 A.D.) or Hemachandra's Prakrit grammar.

The oldest Pali grammar is *Kachchayanaprakarana* written by Katyayana.

Lexicography. Lexicography had its origin in Vedic *Nighantus*, in *Dhatu-pathas* (lists of roots) and *Gana-pathas* (lists of word-groups) and is represented in works like *Amara-Kosa* (*c.* 550-750 A.D.), *Abhidhana-ratna-mala* of Halayudha (*c.* 950 A.D.) and *Abhidhana-chintamani* of Hemachandra.

Philosophy. Philosophy (*Anvikshiki* or *Darsana*) is presented in six systems known as (1) *Purva-mimamsa*, (2) *Uttara-mimamsa*, (3) *Sankhya*, (4) *Yoga*, (5) *Nyaya* and (6) *Vaisesika*, summarised in *Sarva-Darsana-samgraha* by Madhava, brother of Vedic scholar Sayana. The literature of each philosophy consists of a *Sutra* work and its commentaries. These *Sutras* are following: —

(1) *Purva-mimamsa-sutra* of Jaimini with its commentators Sabarasvamin and Kumarila (C 700 A.D.).

(2) *Vedanta-sutra* of Badarayana with the famous Sankara as its commentator (*c.* 800 A.D.). The literature of Vedanta is best represented in such works as the *Karikas of Gauda-*

pada, *Vedanta-sara* of Sadananda (*c.* 1500 A.D.), *Sri-bhashya* of Ramanuja (*c.* 1175-1250 A.D.), and the commentaries of Madhva (1197-1276 A.D.).

(3) *Sankhya-Karika* of Isvarakrishna (translated into Chinese between 557 and 569 A.D.), "the pearl of the whole scholastic literature of India" (Barth), with its commentaries like *Sankhya-tattva-kaumudi* of Vachaspati Misra, or *Sankhya-pravachana-bhashya* by Vijnana-bhikshu (*c.* 1550 A.D.).

(4) *Yoga-sutra* of Patanjali, with its commentary attributed to Vyasa and called *Yoga-bhashya*.

(5) *Nyaya-sutra* of Akshapada Gotama, with its commentary known as *Nyaya-sutra-bhashya* written by Pakshilasvamin Vatsyayana (*c.* 350 A.D.). This *Bhashya* was commented on by Uddyotakara, by Udayana (10th Century A.D.) in his work called *Kusumanjali*, by Dinnaga, Dharmakirti who wrote *Nyayabindu* (c. 800 A.D.), and Hemachandra, author of *Pramana-Mimamsa*. Gangesa founded at Navadvipa in Bengal the system of *Navya-nyaya* (new logic) expounded in his work called *Tattva-chintamani* (c. 1200 A.D.).

(6) *Vaiseshika-sutra* of Kasyapa Kanada, with its *bhashya* called *Padartha-dharma-samgraha* written by Prasastapada (*c.* 700 A.D.); commentary called *Saptapadarthi* written by Sivaditya, and *Tarka-samgraha* of Annam Bhatta.

Law. The works on Law are called *Dharma-sutras* and *Dharma-sastras*. The former belonged to the period 800-300 B.C. These treat more of religious duties and rites than secular law. Examples of *Dharma-sutras* are those of Apastamba (c. 400 B.C.), Baudhayana, Gautama, Vasishtha and Vishnu. Law in general was treated in later works known as the metrical *Dharma-sastras* and *Smritis*, e.g., *Manava-dharma-sastra* or *Manu-smriti*, known for the commentary written on it by the Kashmiri scholar Medhatithi; and *Dharma-sastra* of Yajnavalkya (*c.* 300 A.D.), with its famous commentary called *Mitakshara* written by Vijnanesvara (1050-1100 A.D.). Next followed *Narada-Smriti* which mentions the coin called *Dinara* first known in Gupta inscription of 400 A.D.

Polity. There were works on Polity of which the most famous is the *Arthasastra* of *Kautilya* which F. W. Thomas in *Cambridge History of India*, Vol. I, assigns to the time of Chandragupta Maurya (*c*. 323-299 B.C.). Later works are the *Nitisara* of Kamandaki and *Nitivakyamrita* of the Jain author Somadeva Suri.

A standard treatise on architecture is called *Manasara* (Quintessence of Measurements) and on music, the *Sangita-ratnakara* of Samgadeva, as well as *Samgita-darpana* of Damodara.

Medicine (*Ayurveda*, the science of longevity counted as the fifth Veda). The indigenous system of medicine in India is as old as popular. It has Vedic origins. The *Atharva-veda* mentions diseases like fever, and their remedies, and gives an exact enumeration of the bones of the human body. A similar enumeration is also contained in the *Satapatha Brahmana*. The *Vinaya* texts give an account of the medical education and practice of the physician Jivaka who was appointed by Emperor Bimbisara as physician in attendance on the Buddha. He cured the Buddha of constipation by making him inhale the fragrance of a medicated lotus flower. He cured patients of head disease, fistula (by an ointment), jaundice, and performed surgical operation on the brain and also intestines to free them from entanglements. This account of his successful medical practice is given in the Buddhist canonical work, *Vinaya*, not given to exaggeration like a work of fiction.

The ancient Indian medical treatises are known as the *Samhitas* of Charaka and Susruta and the *Ashtanga-samgraha* of Vagbhata.

An interesting point of Indian Ayurvedic system is that it was introduced to five Hellenistic States of Europe by the Indian emperor Asoka. He despatched to those States his medical missions fully equipped for the humanitarian service of the relief of suffering of all creatures, man and beast (*manushya-chikitsa* and *pasu-chikitsa*). He also equipped the mission with stores of appropriate medicines derived from the three sources of herbs (*aushadha*), roots (*mula*) and fruits (*phala*). This fact is stated by the Emperor in his Rock Ediots II and XIII. (*c.* 260 B.C.). The knowledge of Ayurveda was widely cultivated in India by the wholesome educational provision that it should be a compulsory subject of study up to the Intermediate stage, as described by I-tsing who had to study the subject as a student of Nalanda *Mahavihara*.

Astronomy. Astronomy had Vedic beginnings due to the need of chronological calculations for rituals by observing the phases of the Moon, the course of the Sun, the seasons, and the Zodiac with its many constellations. One of the *Brahmanas* notes that the Sun does not rise and set but produces by its own revolution day and night on earth.

The chief astronomical works are: (1) the *Surya-Siddhanta* as one of the five *Siddhantas* (*Panchasiddhantika*) of Varahamihira (*c.* 505 A.D.); (2) *Aryabhatiya* of *Aryabhata;* (3) *Brahma-sphuta-siddhanta* of Brahmagupta (628 A.D.); (4) *Siddhanta-siromani* of Bhaskaracharya (1150 A.D.).

Mathematics. The astronomical works of Brahmagupta and of Bhaskara record Hindu mathematical achievements in a highly developed form. Besides simple arithmetic, there were known algebra, simple equations, and indeterminate equations of the second degree solved by a method which Hankel describes "as the most delicate operation in the theory of numbers that had been achieved before the time of the great French astronomer Lagrange (of 18th century)."

The study of geometry is traced to the *Sulva-sutras* and the design of the sacrificial ground involving construction of right angles, squares, and circles. The ritual experts had to know how to transform rectangles into squares, into circles, and *vice versa*.

India's literary legacy has been enriched also by modern Indo-Aryan languages. A considerable contribution has been made by the religious songs of saints like Chandidasa (14th century) in Bengali, Vidyapati (15th century) in Maithili, Kabir, and Mira Bai (15th century) in Hindi, Namdeva (13th century) and Tukarama (17th century) in Marathi, Narsingh Mehta (15th century) in Gujarati, Latta (14th century) in Kashmiri, each followed by many successors. We may add to this the Sikh *Granth* and *Ramayana* of Tulsi Das (16th-17th century) as epoch-making works.

CHAPTER XV

POSITIVIST THOUGHT

THIS chapter aims to present an aspect of Indian culture which has not received the attention it deserves. It is the element of posivitist thought which has influenced that culture through the ages. Evidence of this influence has been indicated in some of the previous chapters. It will be useful to sum it up. The spiritual and philosophical aspect of Indian culture has been studied more than its mundane and secular aspects. It is sometimes also assumed that Indian culture is more concerned with the other world than with the interests of this world and its material life. This is a misconception to be removed. It is to be borne in mind that the Republic of India has been planned as a secular State in the sense that it stands equally for all religions and gives them equal freedom for their profession, practice, and preaching. It is because such religious freedom is consistent with the national and social ideals which have inspired and informed Indian culture through the ages, and are not foreign and adventitious to its spirit. It is not something which is derived from the impact on it of modern thought. In fact, a student of Indian culture investigating its principles, contents, and characteristics, will find that a good deal of what now passes as Socialism or Communism is held in solution in some of the traditions and institutions in which that culture expresses itself.

We have, for instance, already seen how some of the Deities worshipped in the *Rigveda* are symbolical of the Welfare State and represent religion as social service, service of man as a mode of worshipping God conceived of as Nara-

Narayana, God-in-Man. The hymn of the *Rigveda* (VIII. 117), as we have seen, is even addressed to the Deity designated as *Dana* or Lilberality, and presents religion as the primary duty of feeding the starving. A later text represents the Deity as manifesting Itself as the elemental craving for food, the Great Hunger which is born with life itself (*Ya devi sarvabhuteshu kshudha rupena samsthita*). It is the highest religion to satisfy that Hunger, which amounts to the gift of life itself. God appears in the form of this Cosmic Hunger. Again, the last hymn of the *Rigveda* prays to God as representing the Common Collective Consciousness of the Community, the National Mind (*Samjnana* or *Samajnana*), with which the Individual Mind must remain in communion as the source of its potency. This Deity may be taken as the Deity of Democracy to be worshipped by its citizens in an integral union of hearts (*chitta*), minds (*manah*), ideals (*akuti*) and policies (*mantra*) so that they may speak with one voice (*samvadadhvam*) at the assemblies where they gather together (*samgachchhaddhvam*). Democracy depends upon moral qualifications, the emotional integration of its votaries.

The *Atharvaveda* again describes the popular bodies as *Sabha* and *Samiti*, as the twin daughters of the Creator whose cosmic purpose they serve as builders of civilization on earth.

The *Vedas* also define and worship God by abstract conceptions such as (1) *Satya* (Truth). "God is to be attained only by Truth;" (2) *Rita* (Cosmic Law); (3) *Sunrita* (Bounty); or (4) *Sraddha* (Faith).

We have also seen how a Vedic hymn (*Rv*. VIII, 79, 2) prays to God as the Saviour of afflicted humanity, "clothing the naked, curing the sick, making the blind see, and the cripple walk."

This Vedic ideal of worshipping God by serving Man was later embodied in a regular religious system which presents

Hinduism as consisting of stages in the progressive expansion of the Individual into the Universal as the ultimate meaning of religion. These stages are described as the compulsory religious obligations to be daily performed by offering worship to God in the five following forms (called *Pancha-Mahayajnas*, the Five Great Sacrifices): Worship of (1) God (*Deva-Yajna*), (2) Ancestry (*Pitri-Yajna*), (3) Rishis as Fathers of Learning, the Makers of Civilization, (4) Man as Guest (*Atithi-Yajna*) or Worship of Humanity represented by the Guest and (5) All Life (*Bhuta-Yajna*) by recognising its sanctity as manifestation of God (*Isavasyam idam sarvam*). Of these five kinds of worship, the first two are directly religious, while the other three are inspired by the ideals of socialism and positivism. They inculcate man's supreme duty and religion to be always to keep alive in gratitude the memory of what he owes to his family and ancestry; to the makers of his national culture and civilization, and the legacy of learning bequeathed to him, a legacy which it is his duty to conserve and extend by his own contributions; to stand up for the continuity of the race; and the culminating recognition of the sanctity of all life in a spirit of Non-violence and Universal Brotherhood as the moral foundation of World Peace.

This socialist and positivist outlook has moulded Hindu religious history through the ages. Hinduism has its centres in temples founded by popular piety and philanthropy. Their endowments contain legal stipulations and provisions not only for the direct religious requirements of ritualistic worship but also for ministering to the social and cultural interests of the community as constituting the background of its spiritual life. A temple was functioning as much as a centre of worship as of learning, especially of Sanskrit study.

Southern India is especially rich in religious endowments providing for both religious and cultural needs of the community. These endowments are recorded in the inscriptions they bear. A few typical epigraphic records may be cited in this connection.

Inscription No. 202 of Madras Epigraphy Report for 1912 registers the gift of land for the maintenance of a Grammar-Hall in the Temple of Tiruvottiyur called *Vyakarana-dana-Vyakhyana-mandapa* by supporting teachers and pupils in their study of Pāṇini's grammar. It shows the liberal cultural outlook of its donor in endowing the study of a hard secular science like grammar as the science of sciences. This School of Grammar achieved great fame and attracted to it further gifts. No. 110 of 1912 registers an agreement by which the residents of a particular locality agreed to pay special tax levied on them for the specific purpose of maintaining this school, while No. 201 records the gift of an entire village made by its proprietor in support of this institution.

No. 182 of 1915 records the benefaction of a Vaisya donor for the establishment of (1) a School for the study of Grammar and the Scriptures, (2) a Hostel for accommodation of students and (3) a Hospital. The Hospital was provided with 15 beds. The staff of the Hostel and Hospital comprised one physician, one surgeon, two menials, two maid-servants as nurses and one general servant for the Hostel and Hospital. The Hospital was also equipped with a store of medicines such as those derived from *Haritaki, Ghrita, Lavana* and some kinds of oil.

No. 518 of 1915 registers the gift made by a queen for the maintenance of a feeding house (*Sattra*) for students and teachers.

Special studies were sometimes endowed. No. 233 of 1911 records a gift for the study of *Prabhakara*, the study of the Mimāṁsa philosophy of Prabhakara. Temples were serving not merely as centres of sacred but also of hard scientific and scholarly study of different schools of philosophy.

No. 259 of 1905 records an endowment of as many as 44 villages for provision of food and clothing for students and teachers and also the entertainment of 54 guests per day, an example of a remarkable secular charity.

The Madras Epigraphy Report for 1917 records another notable example of a secular benefaction in aid of a school, a hospital, and a feeding house and another founding several social institutions such as a feeding house, school, hospital, and a maternity home, besides the usual temple and monastery. We have also record of endowments for equipping a village with a garrison of village-guards for its protection and with the machinery for promoting its economic welfare by settling in the village craftsmen of different kinds, goldsmith, coppersmith, mason, bamboo-worker, blacksmith, potter, architect, carpenter, barber and artisan to make the village a self-sufficient economic unit by itself. The feeding houses were conducted in a spirit of laudable liberality by admitting to its alms men of all castes from Brahmana down to the Chandala.

An inscription found at Nellore records the endowment of the following secular studies: *Rasa, Rasayana, Padanjana, Khadga-yaga, Ghutika* (magic), *Kanyaka-Vada* (erotics), *Mantra-Vada* (spells), *Dhatu-Vada* (metallurgy), *Dhumra-Vada* (art of producting optical illusions in smoke), *Garuda-Vada* (ornithology) and *Rasa-Vada* (chemistry).

The socialist ideal expressed itself not only in religious endowments and texts but also in art. This is seen in a unique sculpture and some paintings decorating the walls of the Minakshi Temple at Madurai. These represent God Siva Himself as taking part in civic obligations for saving the city against the flood of its river making breaches in its embankment. Every citizen was required by its ruler by conscripted labour to collect and carry his quota of earth into the breach. A poor widow in her inability to discharge her obligation prayed to God Siva for help. Her prayer brought down God into the earthly scene where He, with other labourers, is seen carrying on his head the basket of earth to be thrown into the breach of the embankment. The divine youth went about his task in a free and frolicsome manner not liked by the overseer who reported him to the king. The king came on the spot and caned the youth on his back, when lo! the blow fell on the backs of all creatures including babies in the womb, and caused a gaping wound on the back of the arch-culprit, the king. The artist's conceit is that a blow to God and His Cosmic Body (*Virat-Deha*) was a blow to all. The Lord then threw off His disguise as a labourer and received the worship of devout citizens by the offering of *Bilva* leaves. These tiny leaves thrown into the river are seen sailing up the stream against the fury of the flood by the spiritual potency with which they were charged in worship. They tamed the turbulent river and the uncontrolled elements. The painter's technique is shown by figures of fishes and boats indicative of the river.

CHAPTER XVI

OUTLINE OF INDIAN THOUGHT

INDIAN Thought is marked by certain special features which may be taken as its contributions to the culture of mankind and to its spiritual consciousness. These may be described as (1) a philosophic interpretation of experience, (2) certain ideals of life, (3) some particulars principles of social organisation and (4) certain norms and forms of discipline. Apart from these social and ethical contributions, there are also other contributions of Indian Thought to culture, such as the logical apparatus of thinking, scientific concepts and mapping out of the physical world, and the philosophical categories of Being and Knowing.

The Hindu views experience as a homogeneous whole, and breaks it up into subjective and objective, into matter and form. He finds the dualism of mind and body, the pluralism of phenomena, the hierarchies of the categories of Being. He investigates Reality in its various departments, but he never treats the Forms of Thought as Thought in abstraction from Reality.

This synthetic instinct of the Hindu mind is to be contrasted with the analytical and differentiating intellect of the West. The Western mind finds fault with the Hindu for his two opposite weaknesses, viz., too much abstraction on the one hand and too much of concretising on the other. But, in fact, the Hindu holds the scale even between the two aspects. He sees the abstract in the concrete, and the concrete in the abstract, the universal in the particular, and the particular in the universal, ideal in the real and the real in the ideal. Above all, he has a sense of Cosmic Unity which enables him to see the whole in the part and the part in the whole.

The principal Indian interpretations of experience may be singled out as (1) Vedantic, (2) Buddhist and (3) Vaishnavite.

According to Vedantic thought as established by Sankara, the Cosmic Process, Experience in Time, is a process which, for the individual, has had no beginning, but will vanish in the end into Eternity. The Absolute Self, by a spontaneous process, which is eternal in the sense of being timeless, alienates Himself from Himself, and generates an infinitum or indefinitum of individual selves. Each individual, by innate necessity, also heterises the Absolute in the form of his object experience, his world of Reality in Time and Space.

Experience is thus of two grades: (i) Absolute existence and (ii) that which exists for and in another, as the object-world, which possesses only practical Reality (the pragmatist's Reality). This mediate experience is the work of *Maya*, the power of self-alienation, and the Absolute, so working through *Maya*, may be called the Supreme Being, *Isvara*, Creator, Providence, Lord. Creation is a cyclical process. Originating by self-alienation, the individual soul, *jivatma*, sets out in quest of the Self of Self, through varieties of untried being, and successive stages of discipline.

Vedanta also emphasises the principle of individuation (*Ahamkara*) which distinguishes between subject and object in the sphere of thinking and between *meum* and *teum* in the sphere of the practical. It is at once the enjoyer (of pleasure and pain), and as such, subject to natural necessity, and doer or responsible agent (earning merit or demerit), and, as such, subject to the law of its conscious functioning, so long as this is prompted by the desires of individuation. Such desire-prompted acts leave residua, *samskaras*, which are themselves latent, but are capable of being roused by proper stimuli. This cycle of desires, residua, and desires again, this chain of moral causes and effects, this mundane series, constitutes the bondage of the individual self.

There are, again, in the Hindu conception, three moments in our mental life, namely, *Tamas* (inertia or indifference), *Rajas* (activity prompted by individualistic desires) and *Sattva* (the manifestation of the essential Reality). These are all moments of the soul (or psychical continuum) in its bondage. But *Tamas* (Inertia) and *Rajas* (individualistic action from Desire) are the fetters that bind. *Sattva* as the source of selfless activity of the individual prompted by Universalistic or Absolute ends, works towards deliverance or liberation. Through a course of discipline, in *Jnana yoga* (intellectual intuition of the Absolute as the Self of selves), *Sattva* (purity) prevails more and more, and individualistic desires, *Rajas*, is gradually reduced till the individual acts from purely Universalistic or Absolute ends. He is now free from bondage, free from the illusion (*Avidya*) of self-alienation and realises himself as the Absolute Self.

Buddhist thought leaves out the Absolute as the prius of the cosmic series, and drops the hypothesis of self-alienation. It regards *Karma* as a moral necessity, working itself out independently of Providence or personal will. But equally with the Vedantist, the Buddhist distinguishes between an unconditioned something (*Nirvana*) and this conditioned existence, which, however, he considers as wholly phenomenal, momentary and relative, unlike the Vedantist.

Vaishnavism explains the motif of creation as not self-alienation or illusion but the self-giving of the Perfect to fulfil the imperfect, the tenderness of the infinitely great stooping to be infinitely little. The cosmos in its endless forms is the sport (*Lila*) of a divine love. Individuation is not an error to be cancelled, for love could not incarnate itself except in a dual relation and the individual is one term of this relation. The cosmic Reality is not merely pure Being (*Sat*); it is also pure intelligence (*Chit*), and, as such, breaks up into the duality of subject and object. Each of these centres reflects the others. Centre calls unto centre, deep unto deep. This mutual give-and-take implies personality, implies love. The Absolute, then, as the sum total of all experience, is neither unipersonal, nor impersonal, but omnipersonal.

From the Vaishnavic point of view, the bondage of the individual arises not from ignorance or illusion, the defect of intelligence, but from self-aberration (*Vaimukhya*), (the turning away of the self), darkening the reason and tainting the will. The individual loses his soul in sense, spirit in matter. But the divine *Lover* woos the erring individual back to Himself. Not *karma*, nor *jnana* but Love (*Bhakti*) is the source of salvation.

To the Vaishnava the Love of the Lord pursuing His beloved is the constant type and theme of all Nature, all Life. Every little atom vibrates to every other. The cloud and the stream, the star and the flower, the moth and the fire, earth and sky—all endlessly enact and re-enact the story of undying Love. The cosmic process is the pursuit of the Vision of Beauty in earth as in heaven.

The Hindu view of Nature is somewhat unique. He views Nature as a separate and independent entity by herself and not as a mere setting to Man. He appreciates Nature as Nature, in her simplicity, her serenity, her silence, her inexhaustible fertility and variety.

The Hindu's pilgrimages are always to the glacier-clad mountains, the palm-clad seashore, or ocean-isle, or the almost impenetrable depths of hill and jungle, where the tread of the generations of man has scarcely been heard.

The Hindu has his own philosophy of Man and Society. The whole cosmic process in all its ascending stages, from mineral to plant and animal, and from the natural man to the saints and heroes, *Avataras* of humanity, is the Divine

Prakriti made manifest, the inner turned outwards. As every individual soul enacts the divine process, every birth is an Incarnation.

The ultimate ground of all duty to Man and Society in Hindu ethics is this unity of all individual selves in the Absolute, the Self of all selves. The ultimate test of conduct is: How far does it help forward the realisation of *Atman* as the end and consummation of all this cosmic process?

This philosophy leads to the gradation of social values not on the basis of wealth or rank but on inner spiritual progress. Even in the West, from Plato to Comte, the sages and philosophers are given a special place of honour and power in society, provided it is not abused. In India, the corrective was applied in a life of self-denial, poverty, purity, and even living on alms or gifts, which was always enjoined and encouraged. Poverty itself was thus sanctified as an uplifting influence by itself. The Indian thus believes in plain living and high thinking, in the art of simplifying the natural wants instead of multiplying them, so that he may be more self-centred and self-sufficient, with greater leisure for thought and spirituality.

This moral attitude has favoured a social organisation in which is held in solution a good deal of socialism and communism. One such institution is the Hindu joint family based on cooperation mitigating the acerbities of individualism. Western society influenced by Roman jurisprudence lays more stress upon private property, upon creditors' rights as against debtors', and generally, more on rights than on obligations. It may be noted that a communistic and collectivistic sense, with its implied socialisms and humanisms, is stronger and more natural in such a society. Indeed, the basal facts of Indian social and family life furnish occasions for a perpetual discipline in human and social sympathies, and in the repression of the aggressive proprietory instincts of the individual, which render him more selfish and limited in sympathies. Such a social principle purifies domestic life by establishing proper relations between its constituents, parent and child, husband and wife, host and guest, teacher and disciple, master and servant, employer and employed, landlord and tenant, sovereign and subject, a man and his friend, and, generally, between man and fellowman, and man and woman. It may be noted that the great emperor Asoka has repeated in almost all his edicts, this primary religion of the cultivation of proper relations (*samprati-patti*) in the family and domestic circle as the foundation of a cultured society. The great epic *Ramayana* has been planned as a mirror of ideal domestic relations. The Hindu has exalted this fundamental social obligation into religion and ritual in the institution of *Pancha-mahayajnas*, i.e. offering worship to the deity (*Deva-yajna*), to ancestors (*Pitri-yajna*), to the fathers of learning (*Rishi-yajna*), to humanity (*Nri-yajna*) and to all life (*Bhuta-yajna*) in recognition of its essential sanctity. It is, however, to be noted that these social relations now are breaking down before the onslaught of modern thought under which the contractual type threatens to supersede that of status.

Social life centres round certain relationships of life which count as its primary formative factors in the Hindu system. Firstly, there is the relationship of parent and child to which all other relationships are subordinate. It is the product of the original conception of God as Divine Father or Divine Mother symbolising a redeeming, a sacrificial, an interceding love. The Human in the Divine is the Son as the Image of the Father. The Son of God is primarily the Son of Man. The relation of ancestors to posterity, of the past to the present, and of the present to the future in the generations of Man, springs from this source. The Hindu sacrificial commemoration of ancestors in (*Pitri-yajna*) is a bond of social continuity and solidarity.

Hinduism also recognises the romance of married life but it emphasises its other ends, and not merely the fruition of desire. It recognises self-dedication culminating even in the abnegation of separate individuality as the soul of conjugal love. The Hindu system holds that spiritually as well as socially, husband and wife are incomplete, each without the other. Indeed, the cosmic process itself is conceived as the result of the union of the Divine *Prakriti* (Nature) with Divine *Purusha* (Spirit). In man this union is attained in the mystery of conjugal love. But conjugal love is something more than this. The household has the child for its central figure. Conjugal love thus becomes the social sacrament. Duty and sacrifice and social service enter as integral elements into the romance of an otherwise physiological (or spiritual) instinct. Hindu thought repudiates the idea of personal enjoyment as the incentive to marriage. The indissolubility of marriage in the Hindu home has primarily a social origin and significance. The wife enters the *Gotra* of her husband and is adopted into his family. She acquires an interest in the estate of her husband and is her husband's proxy in religious sacraments. This explains the non-transferability of the Hindu widow. There is also the emotional reaction and repulsion to the harrowing spectacle of a change of parents being enacted before the very eyes of the children as its mute and helpless witnesses under the modern legal facilities of divorce. The tragedy amounts to a veritable slaughter of innocents whose future is blighted for no fault of their own, while the law cannot touch the other natural and fixed relationship between brother and sister. Again, the Hindu disapproval of widow remarriage and of free social intercourse between the sexes is not to be considered as any slur on woman but as the outcome, on the contrary, of a romantic devotion to woman and to whatever is supposed to ennoble, refine and purify woman.

It is necessary to elaborate the contribution of Buddhist thought to culture. Buddhism does not set much store by philosophical and metaphysical speculation on fundamental issues and problems such as the Absolute, or the mystery of Creation. It believes that religion is something to be lived, and not merely to be studied or discussed. It believes in the application of religion to life and conduct so that it becomes a second nature. The essence of the Buddha's teachings is contained in the very first teaching of his life as recorded in *Dharma-chakra-pravartana-sutra*. It starts with the four fundamental truths of life, namely, *Dukkha* or suffering as a universal experience, its origin in Desire (*Trishna*), its prevention (*Nirodha*) and the path (*magga*) leading to its cessation. The path is called the Middle Path, the Eight-fold Path (*Atthangika Magga*) which admirably sums up the practical duties and obligations of religious life. These are thus enumerated:

1 Right View (*Samyak Drishti*). Religious life must start with the right assessment and appraisal of the values of life and of their order of priorities so as to differentiate between the permanent and the perishable, true and false. The Buddha himself presented an example of the right *Darsana*, or philosophy of life by renouncing the world with its transient interests to devote Himself to the pursuit of Truth Everlasting.

2. Right Resolve (*Samyak Samkalpa*). Life must be planned according to correct philosophy.

3. Right Speech (*Vak*). Speech must not deviate from life's ideal, which it must not violate.

4. Right Work (*Karma*). The fundamental philosophy of life must control its activities.

5. Right Livelihood (*Ajiva*). A man's occupation shapes his character. The end does not justify the means. Both must be pure and untainted.

6. Right Effort (*Vyayama*). Religious life depends in the words of Asoka's edict upon utmost self-exertion, upon *Abhyasa* as pointed out by Patanjali in his *Yogadarsana*.

7. Right Mindfulness (*Smriti*). One must not be forgetful of, but be always alive to, his duties and obligations which he must take seriously and not listlessly. The product and ultimate outçome of all these seven injunctions and practices is:

8. *Samadhi* or Right Concentration. It is further stated that the culmination of spirituality is Purity of Heart (*chittavisuddhi*) which can be attained only by what is called *Shilavisuddhi* or Purity of Conduct on the basis of the practice of the last three injunctions.

Perhaps the most important contribution of Buddhist thought is its development known as Mahayana, by which it has impressed itself most on certain Asiatic countries which are described in Sanskrit texts as *Dvipantara Bharata*, the India of the islands, aptly called by Zimmer—Indian Asia. The best evidence of Indian influence on these foreign countries conveniently called Greater India is the art of those countries as seen mainly in its sculptures inspired by Mahayana.

The Buddha himself has described Buddhism as a path (*Marga*), Pratipad, leading to Nirvana, end of the constant succession of rebirths. Sometimes it is also described as a vehicle, *yana*, for conveying its passengers to the same goal, "the town or island of *Nirvana*". The first metaphor applies to earlier Buddhism, *Hinayana*, and the second to later Buddhism called Mahayana. The idea is that the earlier Buddhism is an inferior, imperfect, inefficient doctrine of salvation, and is thus dubbed as the "Little Vehicle."

The most noteworthy feature of Great Vehicle or Mahayana is the stress it lays on the path of devotion (*Bhaktimarga*). It is thus the Buddhist form of the Hindu cult of *Bhakti* or Devotion. It may be further noted that while the ideal of ancient Buddhism is the *Arhat* who is "useless" to others and an utter egoist, Mahayana replaces this ideal by the Buddha as the being of compassion and pity and not as the saint for himself, the hero of charity, saving the world at the cost of so many lives consecrated to the world. Mahayana also is marked out by its deification of Buddha, and worship of Buddhas and Bodhisattvas as first depicted in the Gandhara monuments although the worship of the Buddha was also contained in the Hinayana. Mahayana also adds to Buddhism some new characters which somewhat diminish the importance of Sakyamuni as its central character. Among these characters are Maitreya, the future Buddha, more living than Sakyamuni, as also Avalokitesvara, Amitabha, Vairochana, Vajrapani and many others whose specifically Buddhist character is not very marked.

Mahayana dates from the 1st century A.D. and is associated with emperor Kanishka and the two learned scholars Asvaghosha and Nagarjuna. Its main characteristic is the worship of Bodhisattvas or potential Buddhas. It is also known for its code of altruistic ethics which teaches that every man must do good in the interest of the whole world and make over to others any merit which he may acquire by his virtues. It is also marked by habitual worship of images and elaboration of ritual. It is a characteristic doctrine of Mahayanism that men can and should try to become Bodhisattvas. The Bodhisattva prefers the salvation of all beings to his own personal salvation. He refuses the bliss of *Nirvana* till he is able to alleviate the sufferings of others.

Mahayana is based on the doctrine of universal love (*karuna*) for all sentient beings. It thus stands for general salvation and not individual as in Hinayana.

A most significant feature of Mahayana Buddhism is its cult of the Bodhisattva who does not exert himself in religious discipline for the sake of his own weal but for the sake of the spiritual benefit of all his fellow creatures. The Mahayanist conception of Bodhisattvahood aims at mitigating the ruthless mechanical rigidity of the law of *Karma* by the force of *Karuna*. The Hinayanist position is: "Your salvation is exclusively your own business, and whatever sympathy I may have is of no avail. All that I can do toward helping you is to let you see intellectually the way to emancipation." But with the Mahayana Bodhisattva, the case is entirely different. He is all-sympathy, all-compassion, all-love. The essence of Bodhisattvahood is this unselfish devotion to the welfare of his fellow beings for whose emancipation he would not even enter upon the tranquillity of *Nirvana*, as distinguished from the Hinayana principle of self-emancipation. The ideal Bodhisattva combines in himself both Prajna and Karuná, supreme knowledge and universal compassion.

This self-sacrifice of the Bodhisattva for his fellow beings receives expression in the technical religious doctrine of *Parivarta*, the doctrine of "turning over" of one's own merits to others in pursuit of their welfare. Thus while individualism is a feature of Hinayana, that of Mahayana is Universalism. According to this doctrine all the innumerable deeds practised by the Bodhisattva are dedicated to the emancipation of ignorant beings. But both the Buddhist systems agree that all Buddhas were Bodhisattvas in their former lives. As Sakyamuni was a Bodhisattva in his former lives, destined to become a Buddha, so we are all Buddhas. History passes, but the heart persists. The individual called Sakyamuni was a historical figure who may be forgotten in course of time but the sacred chord struck by him in the inmost heart reverberates through eternity.

Nagarjuna in his work on the *Bodhichitta* elucidates the Mahayanist notion of the Bodhisattva as follows:

"The essential nature of all Bodhisattvas is a great loving heart (*Maha-karuna-chitta*) and all sentient beings constitute the object of his love. Therefore, the Bodhisattvas do not cling to the blissful state attained by *Dhyana* or meditation and do not covet the fruit of their own good deeds which may heighten their own happiness. Their great hearts of sympathy never leave suffering creatures behind in their journey towards enlightenment."

Vasubandhu ascribes to the Bodhisattva's attitudes the following:

(1) "Would that all the merits I have accumulated in the past as well as in the present be distributed among all sentient beings, and make them all aspire after supreme knowledge!"

(2) "Would that I all the time accompany and protect all sentient beings and remove from them things which are not beneficial to them!"

In fine, the Bodhisattva while himself living in the highest plane of spirituality chooses to set out in the world of particulars and senses, and, placing himself on the level of his fellow beings, he works, he toils, and suffers like them, and turns over all his merits towards them. The sacred motive that induces the Bodhisattva to renounce a life of Nirvanic self-complacency is nothing but his boundless love for all beings. Love is that which stimulates a man to go beyond his own interests. It is the mother of all Buddhas and Bodhisattvas.

The following passage from Devala's *Mahapurusha* explains this point very well:

Nirvana in truth consists in rejoicing at others being made happy, and *Samsara* is not so feeling. He who feels a universal love for all his fellow creatures will rejoice in distributing blessings among them and find his *Nirvana* in so doing. How can the Bodhisattva enter into *Nirvana* by leaving behind him his fellow-beings whose sufferings he feels as his own in himself?"

This Buddhist sentiment of universal love is the root of all religions and their unity.

There is also an interesting passage from a *Mahayana-sutra*. When Vimalakirti was asked why he did not feel well, he made the following reply:

"As all sentient beings are ill, so am I ill. When all sentient beings are healed of their illness, I shall be healed of my illness too. Why? The Bodhisattva loves all sentient beings as his own children. When they are sick, he is sick too. The illness of the Bodhisattva comes from his all-embracing love."

The following prayer is daily recited in Mahayana temples and monasteries: "Sentient beings, however innumerable, I take vow to save."

Nirvana is no negation of life, nor is it an idle contemplation on the misery of existence. It means a total consecration of the emancipated being to the deliverance of all his fellow beings.

It will be thus seen that, on the whole, Indian Thought in its particular phase and development known as *Mahayana* anticipates the most modern and positivist thought and outlook on life.

It may also be noted that while *Mahayana* elaborates and emphasises the ideal of the Bodhisattva, its origins are to be found in Hinayana and early Buddhist scriptures. The Bodhisattva stands for the two primary virtues called *Mahamaitri* and *Mahakaruna*. *Maitri* is love of all living beings like the mother's love of her only son. *Karuna* is the compassion which moves the Bodhisattva to seek enlightenment first not for himself but for others. His prayer is: 'May I become a Buddha to effect the good and happiness of all, sentient beings, and to make amend of all kinds of their sufferings!' The crowning statement is contained in the *Vinaya Pitaka* [Mahavagga I and II], stating that the Blessed One addressed the following words of exhortation to the Bhikkhus after His attainment of Enlightenment:

"I am delivered, O Bhikkhus, from all fetters, human and divine. You, O Bhikkhus, are also delivered from all fetters. Go ye now, and wander (*charata*), O Bhikkhus, on missions of social service for the gain, the good, and welfare of all, both men and gods (*Charatha Bhikkave charikam Bahujananahitaya=bahujana sukhaya=Athhaya Hitaya sukhaya Devamanussanam*)." This soul-stirring message of social service inspired the Buddhist missionaries in their work for the spread of their faith in foreign lands so as to build up a Greater India beyond the bounds of India.

INDEX

ILLUSTRATIONS

Examples of Neolithic Ruddle Drawings showing Stag, Crocodile, Boar and hunters.

Interior of a Delwada Jain Temple, Mount Abu.

Ajatasatru worshipping the Buddha.

Rock-cut "rathas", Mamallapuram.

Sun Temple, Konarak.

Trimurti, Elephanta.

Kalyanasundara, Ellora.

Dream of Mayadevi, Bharhut.

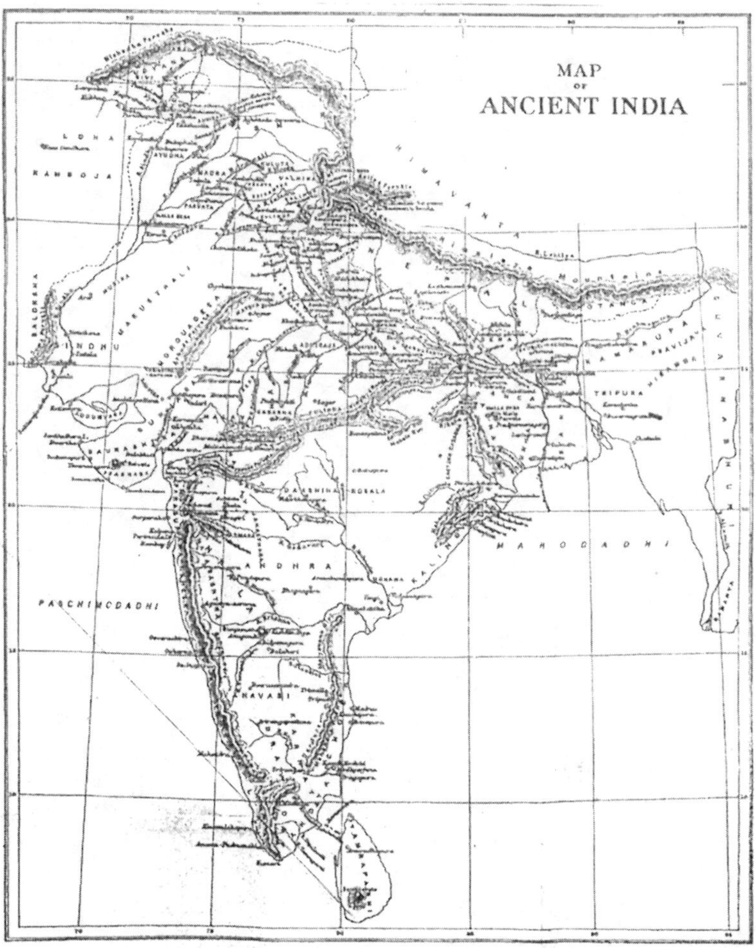
MAP
OF
ANCIENT INDIA
HIMAVANTA
KAMBOJA
TRIPURA
DAKSHINA KOSALA
ANDHRA
MAHODADHI
PASCHIMODADHI